W9-CVP-871

The Compact Guide to
Tort Law
A Civilized Approach to the Law

The Compact Guide to
Tort Law
A Civilized Approach to the Law

Jefferson Hane Weaver
Attorney at Law

WEST PUBLISHING COMPANY
St. Paul   New York   Los Angeles   San Francisco

Composition by Parkwood Composition Services, Inc.
Copyediting by Kathy Pruno
Cover Image by Lee Sievers
Cover Design by Kristin Weber
Indexing by Schroeder Editorial Services

Printed in United States of America
97 96 95 94 93 92 91 90   8 7 6 5 4 3 2 1 0

Library of Congress Cataloging-in-Publication Data

Weaver, Jefferson Hane
    *The Compact Guide to Tort Law: A Civilized
    Approach to the Law* / Jefferson Hane Weaver
        p.   cm.
    Includes index.
    ISBN 0-314-81728-X
    1. Torts—United States   I. Title
KF1250.Z9W36   1991
346.7303—DC20   90-23101
[347.3063]   CIP ∞

This book is dedicated to
Britt Lockwood Weaver,
Todd Howard Weaver,
and Russell Lea Weaver.

About the Author

Jefferson Hane Weaver received his B.A. from the University of North Carolina at Chapel Hill and his J.D. from the Columbia University School of Law in New York City. He also received his M.A. and his M.Phil. from the Columbia University Graduate School of Arts and Sciences, where he is now completing his Ph.D. He has written *The World of Physics* (3 volumes) and *The Compact Guide to Contract Law*. He has also coauthored with Lloyd Motz *The Concepts of Science, The Story of Physics, The Atomic Scientists*, and *The Unfolding Universe*. He currently practices law in Fort Lauderdale, Florida, where he resides with his wife, Shelley Jo, and their two children, Mark Christopher Louis and Catharine Emily Hane.

CONTENTS

Foreword

Although torts is regarded by many students as the most entertaining of legal subjects, it is sometimes presented in a manner that is dull and unimaginative. Many people have still managed to grasp the fundamental concepts of torts, but they have probably wondered if there was some way in which they might have been introduced to its basic principles without having to wade through long-winded explanations and dusty cases. Although repetition is often the best way to commit particular ideas to memory or at least better understand those ideas, the subject of torts—like many other legal topics—is sometimes rendered inaccessible to the student because it is taught in a manner that emphasizes its details instead of the overall structure of the subject itself.

The Compact Guide to Tort Law, like the other books in this series, is a summary that is intended to provide the reader with a general understanding of the basic concepts of torts. It is a supplementary reading—not a textbook—that can be used to help the reader clarify such terms as *negligence* or *defamation*. Because I have tried to make this book entertaining to read, I have employed original examples to illustrate particular points. Although some persons may find these examples to be bizarre or absurd, I believe that such an approach will enable the reader to comprehend the fundamental elements of tort law much more easily. Such an approach is admittedly at odds with the way in which torts is usually taught. The fact that I have chosen to use humorous examples to illustrate the basic concepts of tort law does not mean that I do not respect my subject; instead I have merely tried to develop another way in which to explain better the workings of that subject.

Because this book is intended to provide a narrative summary of tort law, it does not make reference to particular legal cases. Its length also necessitates that the various legal principles presented within it be illustrated in such a manner that might make the law appear more simplistic and less deliberative than it is in reality. It is not my desire to create the impression that a particular factual pattern will necessarily give rise to a specific outcome, but it is possible that such an impression may be created at various points within this book owing to its abbreviated length. In the real world, the law is much less predictable and automatic. Moreover, the basic principles of tort law, like many other areas of jurisprudence, have evolved in fits and starts over several centuries and, consequently, have a much richer history than could be told in a book of this size.

Because this book purports to be a brief summary of tort law, it is necessarily dependent on a number of other sources. Some of the other books on which I relied for guidance and clarification in writing

Foreword

The Compact Guide to Tort Law include the follow-
ing: Jerome A. Barron, *Public Rights and the Private
Press*. Toronto: Butterworths, 1981; Kenneth S. De-
vol, *Mass Media and the Supreme Court*, 3d ed. New
York: Hastings House, 1982; Graham Douthwaite,
Attorney's Guide to Restitution. Indianapolis: Allen
Smith Co., 1977; John G. Fleming, *The American
Tort Process*. Oxford: Clarendon Press, 1988; Leon
Green, *The Litigation Process in Tort Law*. Char-
lottesville: Michie Company, 1977; Fowler K. Har-
per, Fleming James, Jr., and Oscar S. Gray, *The Law
of Torts*, 2d ed. Boston: Little Brown & Co., 1986;
Barry S. Josephson, *Torts*. Culver City: Josephson/
Kluwer Legal Educational Centers, Inc., 1986; Ed-
ward J. Kionka, *Torts: Injuries to Persons and Prop-
erty*. St. Paul: West Publishing Co., 1977; William
M. Lande and Richard A. Posner, *The Economic
Structure of Tort Law*. Cambridge: Harvard Univer
sity Press, 1987; Slade R. Metcalf, *Rights and Lia-
bilities of Publishers, Broadcasters, Reporters*. New
York: Shepherd's/McGraw-Hill, Inc., 1989; Dix W.
Noel and Jerry J. Phillips, *Products Liability*. St. Paul:
West Publishing Co., 1981; Joseph A. Page, *The Law
of Premises Liability*. Cincinnati: Anderson Publish-
ing Co., 1976; Robert H. Phelps and E. Douglas Ham-
ilton, *Libel*, rev. ed. New York: Dover, 1978; William
L. Prosser, *Handbook of the Law of Torts*, 4th ed. St.
Paul: West Publishing Co., 1971; Robert L. Rabin,
Perspectives in Tort Law, 2d ed. Boston: Little Brown
& Co., 1983; Robert D. Sack, *Libel, Slander and Re-
lated Problems*. New York: Practicing Law Institute,
1980; Bruce W. Sanford, *Libel and Privacy*. Engle-

wood Cliffs: Prentice-Hall, 1985; Victor E. Schwartz, *Comparative Negligence*, 2d ed. Indianapolis: Allen Smith Co., 1986; Stuart M. Speiser, Charles F. Krause, and Alfred W. Gans, *The American Law of Torts*. Rochester: Lawyer's Cooperative Publishing Co., 1983; Allen F. Westin, *Privacy and Freedom*. New York: Atheneum, 1967; G. Edward White, *Tort Law in America*. Oxford: Oxford University Press, 1980; Harry L. Zuckerman and Martin J. Gaynes, *Mass Communications Law*, 2d ed. St. Paul: West Publishing Co., 1983.

Jefferson Hane Weaver
July 18, 1990

The Compact Guide to
Tort Law
A Civilized Approach to the Law

CHAPTER 1

Intentional Torts

Now this is the Law of the Jungle—as old and as true as the sky.

— Rudyard Kipling

1

Introduction

We used to live in a simpler time in which a trespasser could be drawn and quartered or a thief's hand cut off without worrying about nitpicky details such as trials or evidence. The development of the modern state, however, has been accompanied by a growing concern for such things as civil rights, which has, in the opinion of some observers, greatly reduced the efficiency with which the courts can dispense justice. In any event, one must accept the fact that an entire body of law has developed to provide procedural and substantive precedents for that group of civil offenses known as torts.

What is a tort? *Black's Law Dictionary,* the most famous legal reference work (which is so comprehensive that it includes many words that no one uses anymore), defines a tort as "a private or civil wrong or injury, other than breach of contract, for which the court will provide a remedy in the form of an action for damages."[1] However, this definition is somewhat qualified because "there must always be a violation of some duty owing to plaintiff, and generally such duty must arise by operation of law and not by mere agreement of the parties."[2] Although we may believe we have already learned something about torts, we must jump feetfirst into the quagmire and begin familiarizing ourselves with the particulars of this subject so as to gain a greater understanding of its fundamental concepts.

Torts is one of the most entertaining areas of the law because it focuses on some of the nasty things that people do to other people and the ways in which these wrongdoers or "tortfeasors" are dealt with by the legal system. The body of law dealing with torts arose as it became clear that many persons commit offenses for which they cannot be prosecuted as criminals because they lack the requisite criminal intent. Moreover, many of those offenses arise from the failure of these persons to perform some existing duty or obligation. In short, there must be some duty owed by one individual to another before a claim founded in tort can be made by the injured party. This precondition that a duty exist restricts the range of offenses that may be considered torts. Fortunately for the ladies and gentlemen who are always within a stone's throw of an ambulance, there is still a great

---

[1] *Black's Law Dictionary,* 5th ed. (St. Paul: West Publishing Company, 1979), 1335.

[2] *Black's,* 1335.

variety of tortious offenses ranging from intentional torts to the person and negligence to defamation and product liability.

Intentional Torts to the Person

What are the legal ramifications of committing intentional torts against the persons of others? What are the ingredients that must exist in a particular instance before the wrongdoer will incur liability for an intentional tort? All intentional torts consist of three parts, the absence of any one of which will sink any attempt to charge the wrongdoer with an intentional tort. First, the wrongdoer must commit an offensive act. Second, the offensive act must be accompanied and motivated by the wrongdoer's conscious intent that the offensive act take place. Third, the wrongdoer's conduct must actually cause the outcome that forms the basis for the tort.

The requirement that there be an act involves only those acts committed by the wrongdoer that are deliberate or purposeful. Acts that result from an unforeseeable event or that originate with the volitional behavior of a third party will not be within the ambit of our definition. I might trip over my sleeping Aunt Agatha while creeping around her bedroom in search of naughty Victorian-era undergarments for a scavenger hunt in which I am competing. In such a case, my striking you (my scavenger hunt partner) as I desperately tried to break my fall would be considered to be a deliberate act even though I threw my arms out as a reflex. Such an action would be regarded as a conscious effort on my part to soften the impact of my landing even though my action was prompted by a reflexive response. On the other hand, if I began coughing uncontrollably after taking a deep whiff of the flowery perfume that pervades Aunt Agatha's bedchambers like a shroud of mist in a rain forest, my striking you while coughing violently would probably not be regraded as a purposeful act even though it is arguably no less deliberate than a reflexive act. To carry our analysis one step further, if you happened to trip over Aunt Agatha's prized cat, Muffy, and you then bumped into me, thereby causing me to topple over and land on Aunt Agatha, I would probably not be held responsible for the act because the chain of events that resulted in Aunt Agatha being injured by her beloved nephew originated with your tripping over the cat.

The question of intent must also be resolved before one can determine whether a tortious offense has been committed. For intentional torts, the requisite intent may be either general or specific. General intent means that the wrongdoer intends to cause the consequences of his actions if he knows with substantial certainty that these consequences will result from his actions. If I offer to play catch with my bratty ten-year-old nephew, Elvin, but I throw the baseball at him as hard as I can to see whether Elvin has the ability to be a major league catcher, I would probably be found to have possessed the general intent to commit the tort of battery if I hit him with the baseball. Even though it was not my conscious desire to bean Elvin, my throwing the ball to him at such an excessive speed suggests that I knew he could not catch the baseball and that it was substantially certain that he would get hurt. Specific intent, on the other hand, means that the wrongdoer intends to cause the consequences of his actions if it is his conscious objective to bring about these consequences. I would be found to have the specific intent for battery if it was my conscious desire to hit Elvin with a baseball even though I might feel that my actions were more than justified given all the times he had pointed out my shortcomings in great detail to my Aunt Agatha. A finding of liability for most intentional torts depends on whether the wrongdoer intended to bring about the consequences that provide the basis for that particular tort.

Transferred intent is a legal concept that often arises in situations where the wrongdoer has acted in a manner that is neither deliberate nor knowing. The most common situation involves the transfer of intent to commit a tort between victims. If I hide in the closet of Aunt Agatha's bedchamber with the intent of giving her a good scare when she opens the door, the fact that her butler, Charles, opens the door to retrieve one of her evening cloaks and is given the scare of his life will not prevent me from being held liable for assault even though I intended to scare Aunt Agatha. I will be liable to Charles because he is the one who suffered the injury caused by my leaping out of the closet and shrieking "Boo!" My intent to scare Aunt Agatha is thus transferred to Charles, the recipient of the injury.

A similar legal fiction is employed in the transfer of torts when the wrongdoer intends to commit one type of tort but her actions result in another type of tort. One example would be if you swung your golf club at my head with the intent of causing me to fear for my well-being (assault). If you miscalculated your swing and actually hit me over the head with your club (battery), then you would be found to have possessed the intent to commit battery even though you merely intended to make me flinch by swinging the club near my head. Although my plea that you be sent to the nearest French penal colony due to your antisocial behavior would probably be ignored, you would still be liable for the more serious offense of battery. Furthermore, you would not be able to avoid liability if you hired a young child to swing the golf club at my head because minors and incompetents may also be held to possess the requisite intent if they commit intentional torts.

Causation is the third and final element in an intentional tort. The defendant's actions must have actually caused the consequences that form the basis for the intentional tort. The wrongdoer must have either acted in a manner that causes the injury or set into motion a chain of events that results in the injury. Because causation problems arise mostly in issues of negligence, a detailed discussion of causation is deferred until the chapter on negligence. However, if there is no causal link between the wrongdoer's actions and the injury suffered by the plaintiff, then it will not be possible to sustain an intentional tort cause of action. In any event, the causation requirement will be met if the defendant's actions are a substantial factor in causing the injury to the plaintiff. If my jumping out of the closet startles Charles so much that he faints and hits his head on a statue of Aunt Agatha's prized cat, Whiskers, my behavior would be deemed to be a substantial factor in causing the mild concussion suffered by Charles. I would be liable even though Charles might be subject to periodic fainting spells owing to his constant exposure to the aromatic blanket pervading Aunt Agatha's bedchambers. Whether he might have fainted at that point owing to the aforementioned susceptibility is not the issue because my startling Charles by my behavior arguably could have caused him to faint because it immediately preceded the fainting.

Now that we have familiarized ourselves with the basic components of intentional torts, we should explore some of the particular torts themselves so that we will have some idea as to what is meant by such terms as *assault, battery,* and *false imprisonment.* Because many of us must deal with the rough-and-tumble conditions of urban living on a daily basis, it is perhaps most appropriate to begin our discussion with the intentional tort of battery.

A battery consists of (1) a deliberate act by a wrongdoer that is done with (2) the intent to touch another person and (3) that results in offensive or harmful contact with the other person. One does not have to be an overachiever in mayhem and run down his intended victim with a steamroller to be found guilty of battery because the focus is on the fact that an intentional harmful or offensive contact has occurred. Although being flattened by a steamroller would arguably be less advantageous than being touched by a feather, both situations could give rise to liability for battery if they were both accompanied by the requisite intent.

As a precondition to a battery offense, the act committed by the defendant must be deliberate and result in a harmful or offensive contact. Although a person desiring to commit a battery to augment her resumé of lifetime achievements could strike another person with her hand or a stick, she might also commit battery in a less overt manner by throwing a horseshoe at her intended victim. In other words, the wrongdoer does not actually need to touch the intended victim to commit a harmful or offensive contact. This less direct form of battery is especially recommended for the more timid wrongdoer who does not wish to be within reach of her enraged victim after she strikes.

The defendant may also be held liable for battery if his actions set into motion a chain of events that results in a harmful or offensive contact with another person. If I take my pet armadillo out for a stroll and I spot Miss Tuttleworth, the neighborhood busybody, walking down the other side of the street, my barking out an attack command to my armadillo that causes him to waddle over to Miss Tuttleworth and begin gnawing at her ankle will cause me to be liable for battery. Even though I did not personally touch Miss Tuttleworth, my attack command was the catalyst that ultimately caused her to suffer armadillo bite marks around her ankle. The fact that my armadillo is traumatized by the incident and refuses to obey my attack commands again (thereby wasting several hundred dollars in attack armadillo lessons) is irrelevant and will not affect my own liability.

The wrongdoer must commit the act with the intent of causing an offensive or harmful touching. In other words, did the wrongdoer commit the act with the objective of causing the offensive contact (specific intent) or did the wrongdoer act in a way so that it was substantially certain that the offensive contact would occur (general intent)? In either case, the intent will be sufficient to support liability for battery. Even if the wrongdoer only intended to frighten the victim by, for example, swinging a golf club near her head, the necessary intent will be imputed to support a charge of battery if the harmful or offensive contact actually occurs.

Less clear is what actions may constitute a harmful or offensive touching. One does not actually need to touch another person to cause a harmful or offensive contact. It will be sufficient if the wrongdoer touches something closely associated with the person such as his clothing or a walking cane. If you run up to a college student and pull his credit cards out of his pocket and toss them onto the ground to demonstrate your disgust with the materialism of the modern world, you have committed a battery because you touched something intimately associated with that student's person in an offensive manner. On the other hand, you would not be liable for battery if you kicked one end of the bench on which the student was seated because the bench is not so intimately associated with the student's physical presence.

Chapter 1

The victim of a battery does not need to be aware of the offensive contact because the entreprenurial wrongdoer can commit a battery even if the victim is unconscious. If I go out for a stroll with my new attack armadillo (who has distemper and rabies so as to ensure that it is always in tip-top fighting condition) and I spot Miss Tuttleworth sleeping in a hammock in her front yard, my command that my beast attack her will render me liable for battery even though she is not awake when my valiant animal pounces on her exposed ankle. It is the fact that an intentional harmful or offensive contact has occurred and not the victim's awareness or apprehension of the same that is crucial to the finding of liability for battery. Yet even if my armadillo does no real harm to Miss Tuttleworth and merely makes a nest for itself in her hair, a charge of battery can still be sustained.

Whether the contact itself will be found to be offensive will depend on what society generally regards as permissible contact. If it is a popular local custom to sic armadillos on persons sleeping in hammocks, then my conduct might not be regarded as objectionable because it falls within the ambit of what is socially acceptable. By the same token, if Miss Tuttleworth is the only person in the area who does not like having an armadillo leap on her while she is sleeping in her hammock, then her undue sensitivity to this particular bestial greeting will probably make it impossible for her to sustain an action for battery. The standard to be considered is whether society as a whole—not one or two of its

Chapter 1

more eccentric members—considers the contact to be repugnant in some way.

Another consideration for the prospective batterer is that he will be responsible for any injuries or damages that result from his actions even if they are not foreseeable. My expectation in ordering my armadillo to attack Miss Tuttleworth is that the animal will frighten her and perhaps take a nip out of her leg. There might be a small flesh wound and some high-pitched shrieks but little else with which to be concerned. Imagine my surprise if, after my armadillo leaped onto the hammock, Miss Tuttleworth jerked up to a sitting position so violently that she cracked three vertebrae in her back, thereby eliminating any possibility that she would ever play professional volleyball. Whether or not a volleyball career was in the cards, the cracked vertebrae were not an injury that could have reasonably been anticipated by myself when I ordered my armadillo to invade the hammock. Nevertheless, I will be responsible for this injury because I am liable for all direct consequences of my actions. Even though Miss Tuttleworth's back injury is something that I could not have foreseen and may be due to an unknown physical impairment, I will have to compensate her for these injuries. This so-called eggshell skull rule applies to all intentional torts and means that the wrongdoer takes the injured party as she finds him, regardless of whether the victim has any unknown physical weaknesses.

There are a number of defenses that will negate any liability for battery that are also applicable to assault and false imprisonment. If the victim consents to a harmful or offensive contact perpetrated by the wrongdoer, then the victim will be precluded from asserting any claim against the wrongdoer for his injuries. Consent may be actual, express, or implied. Actual consent is the most direct form of consent and could consist of nothing more than the following statement: "I agree to permit you to pummel me mercilessly because I enjoy the attention." Such a statement indicates that the victim has given his consent to an action that would otherwise constitute a battery. Express consent, on the other hand, is evidenced not by a statement of consent but by actions indicating that the person had consented to the contact. If I participate in a contact sport such as pig wrestling, I have essentially agreed to waive any legal rights I might have against the owners of the pig for any injuries the pig inflicts on me. Whether or not I believe I have given my consent is irrelevant because the focus will be on whether the circumstances were such that it was reasonable for the owner of the pig to believe that I had given my consent. Because I voluntarily stepped into the ring with the pig, my consent will be presumed to have been given. By contrast, if I am unconscious and need to be given lifesaving medical care, my consent for such care will be implied under the law. If there was no provision for implied consents in such situations, then ungrateful accident victims who received emergency medical treatment while unconscious would be able to sue their benefactors for battery because they were not able to consent to being given lifesaving treatment.

Chapter 1

The validity of a person's consent will often depend on whether that person had sufficient information to make an informed judgment. In other words, the consent may not be valid if the consenting party did not know all the relevant facts before giving consent. If I agree to undergo an appendectomy but my doctor fails to inform me that she will be using a novel surgical technique that will subject me to a significant risk of developing salesman's bravado (a rare speech impediment in which the speaker is compelled to describe everything in superlative terms), my consent will be negated insofar as it relates to my doctor's liability for the speech impediment. Consequently, she will incur liability only if I develop the speech impediment because I did consent to the appendectomy itself.

A different situation would arise if the doctor decided, while performing the appendectomy, that it would be advisable to rearrange some of my internal organs. Because this rearrangement was not contemplated when I gave my consent to the appendectomy, such a procedure would arguably be outside the scope of my consent. However, that problem might not pose a significant obstacle if I had signed a consent form giving the doctor blanket authorization to do whatever she felt was necessary to perform the appendectomy. If I did not give such an open-ended authorization, then my doctor's ventures outside the scope of my consent will be privileged only if the situation is such that a reasonable person would have consented to the additional surgery under the circumstances and the unauthorized actions will facilitate the successful completion of the operation itself. If I agreed to permit only the appendectomy, however, and not any additional surgery—regardless of whether my life was endangered—then if my doctor performed additional surgical procedures after finishing the appendectomy, she would be liable for battery because I did not consent to the physical invasion of my person beyond the appendectomy itself.

The participants in a brawl may also consent to any harmful or offensive contacts unless a statute exists prohibiting such altercations, which makes it impossible for the participants to give their legal consent and thus escape liability for battery. If I finally reach my limits of patience with an eighty-year-old crossing guard (who always seems to take particular delight in stopping my car at his intersection) and I leap out of my car to challenge him to battle, his participation in the fight will not necessarily protect me from liability for battery if I bloody his nose. The relevant law may void any actual or express consent given by the crossing guard's agreement to fight me. In the absence of such a legal prohibition, the crossing guard's consent to participate in battle might be void if he did not have the ability to comprehend the consequences of his actions or if his participation was prompted by coercion or fraud. If the crossing guard was of borderline mental competence and was incapable of understanding that I wanted to punch him in the nose, then his consent would be regarded as invalid and I would still be liable for battery. Similarly, if the crossing guard agreed to battle me only because I waved a large stick at him in a menacing manner or I told him that I was an actor and that we would be staging a fight only for the benefit of a hidden camera, then his consent to any injuries he receives from the fighting would be invalid because he was forced against his will to participate or was fraudulently induced by my false statements to agree to fight me.

A person may also defend himself from attack by another and not incur any liability for battery. This right of self-defense arises only if the aggressor has acted in such a way that the other party reasonably believes that the aggressor intends to harm him and that only the use of force will prevent such an attack. The claim of self-defense will not be available to the aggressor if he was the one who originally attacked the other party and the other party responded with force to protect himself. If I was feeling particularly masculine and wished to impress my adoring female companion, the lovely and morally ambiguous Ingrid Engebrettsen, then my starting a fight with the crossing guard would cause me to be branded the aggressor. If the crossing guard was a former champion boxer and began pummeling me without mercy, I would not be able to claim self-defense if I managed to knock him unconscious with a stick. I was the one who started the fight; the fact that the crossing guard gave me a sound thrashing would not enable me to claim that I swatted him with the stick in self-defense because his punching me was prompted solely by my attacking him.

The crossing guard would be able to claim the right of self-defense only so long as it was reasonably necessary for him to protect himself from my aggressive tactics. If he managed to land an uppercut that knocked me unconscious, then he would no longer have the right to use force against me because I could not possibly harm him. Consequently, the crossing guard's desire to plant a few gratuitous kicks in my midsection would not be privileged because I no longer posed any threat to his physical well-being. Similarly, the crossing guard's response to my initial aggression must be reasonable and proportionate. If I take a swing at him, he will be privileged if he responds in kind to protect himself. However, if he retrieves a bazooka and begins firing shells at me, his conduct will not fall within the ambit of self-defense because it is clearly excessive when compared with the force that I originally used against him. Furthermore, the use by the crossing guard of a weapon such as a bazooka or even a pistol would raise the ante beyond the privilege of self-defense because he would be using deadly force to respond to what most people would consider nondeadly force. Many states permit a person to use deadly force to respond to nondeadly force only if there is no way for that person to retreat from the scene without endangering his own safety. However, this rule of retreat does not apply when one is in one's home and responding to the threats posed by an intruder. As far as the crossing guard is concerned, his use of deadly force might be privileged if he is in fact a feeble old man whose life could be threatened by even a single punch. On the other hand, if he is a vigorous former champion boxer who could easily take care of me without resorting to firearms, then his use of the bazooka would probably fall outside the privilege of self-defense.

A person may also defend a third party from the attacks of an aggressor and avoid any liability for battery. However, the intervening party "stands in the shoes" of the party whom he is defending and may use only that amount of force that the apparent victim was privileged to use. In other words, if the person being defended was actually the original aggressor, then the intervening party will not have any greater rights to defend that person than could have been exercised by that person on his own behalf. Consequently, if the crossing guard was punching me with various left-right combinations in response to my original swing at his head, then the intervention on my behalf by Ingrid Engebrettsen in the form of a well-placed kick to the groin of the crossing guard will not be privileged because I was the one who started the fight. This outcome presupposes that the crossing guard would not be using excessive force in response to my original roundabout right. If the crossing guard had knocked me unconscious and was continuing to batter me with his fists, then Ingrid's kick would be privileged because the crossing guard's actions were now beyond the scope of self-defense and more along the lines of sadistic bloodletting. Similarly, the crossing guard's use of deadly force in response to my aggressive behavior would cause him to exceed his privilege of self-defense and thus give Ingrid the right to use her spiked heels on my behalf.

One may also use force to protect one's property, but it must be reasonable under the circumstances. Moreover, one can never use deadly force to protect property itself; such force may be used only in conjunction with efforts to protect another person's physical well-being. If I was a collector of handheld stop signs and I grabbed the crossing guard's stop sign when he refused to donate it to my collection, he would be privileged to use only nondeadly force to recover his stop sign. In short, he could tackle me and punch me a few times if such actions were required for him to regain possession of his stop sign. However, he would not be able to retrieve his bazooka and focus it on my receding figure to prevent me from escaping with his property because he would be using deadly force to protect his property. This is not to say that the crossing guard cannot take whatever reasonable measures are necessary to prevent my absconding with his property but only that he cannot use deadly force to prevent the same. Moreover, the crossing guard must first request that I return the sign before he can use force unless the circumstances indicate that such a request would be pointless.

Although the terms *assault* and *battery* are often used interchangeably, there is a significant difference between the two terms. An assault is committed when (1) the wrongdoer consciously acts (2) with the intent that the intended victim fear that she will suffer a harmful or offensive contact (3) which actually causes the intended victim to fear that she will suffer such contact. Hence, the tort of assault deals not with the contact itself but with the apprehension of the contact that is created in the mind of the intended victim by the acts of the wrongdoer.

Chapter 1

The act that creates the apprehension must involve some sort of physical action such as brandishing a knife or a gun. In general, verbal threats alone are not usually regarded as sufficient to create the apprehension in the mind of the intended victim that she is in danger of suffering immediate injury. However, threatening words coupled with the pointing of a semiautomatic weapon at the intended victim will be regarded as an assault because the weapon adds an element of physical coercion to the verbal threats. Words alone might be sufficient to commit an assault if the aggressor is a huge, powerful man and the victim is an elderly lady because it is reasonable to suppose that the elderly lady would fear for her safety if threatened by such a bully. If, on the other hand, the elderly lady always carried a razor-tipped walking stick and was capable of slicing the most powerful thug to ribbons with a few snaps of her wrist, then it is less likely that the thug could actually commit an assault because such a woman probably would not fear any aggressor. Because the law focuses on acts that would cause apprehension in a reasonable person, however, an assault would be committed in most cases in which threatening words were accompanied by some physical act such as aiming a gun.

The wrongdoer must actually intend to cause the victim to fear that she will be subject to harmful or offensive contact in the immediate future to commit an assault. If I go for a walk around my block and I take my hedge trimmer with me to fend off any hostile dogs I may encounter on my journey, the fact that Miss Tuttleworth sees me coming with my trimmer in hand and believes that I plan to dismember her in the very near future will not result in my being held liable for assault because I did not intend to take portions of Miss Tuttleworth back home with me. My only thought was to take a walk along the street and wave the hedge trimmer at any dog that tried to take liberties with my legs. However, I would be liable for assault if I waved the hedge trimmer in a threatening manner at Miss Tuttleworth and caused her to fear for her safety even though I did not intend to harm her and was only playing a cruel joke on my neighbor.

The apprehension of impending harm must be reasonable because some people believe that everybody wants to harm them. Although different people have different ideas as to what level of anxiety would be reasonable, the necessary apprehension will be presumed to have been introduced into the mind of the intended victim by the wrongdoer if the aggressor demonstrates that he has the ability to carry out the particular threat. After all, if we tried to lock up all the persons who the typical paranoid psychotic believes are intent on causing him to fear for his personal safety, then there would be very few people left outside the jails. Fortunately, we live in a society that believes in locking up paranoid psychotics so that the rest of us may freely go about our business exercising our rights to intimidate anyone we choose.

To constitute an assault, the threat of harm must be immediate. If the threat is made in a manner that indicates it will occur in the distant future or only after certain conditions have occurred, then it will not be considered to be sufficiently immediate to be an assault. If I threaten to wrap my golf club around the neck of the crossing guard when the local high-school basketball team (the dynastic floormat of its conference) wins the championship, then the threat of harm is too far in the future to be considered an assault. Similarly, my conditioning my golf club twisting on the occurrence of a certain event such as the explosion of the sun will cause the threat to be regarded as too remote to be an assault. Further-more, the threat will not be sufficient if the wrong-doer is too far away to commit the particular act or if he has not reached the stage in his preparation where the threat can actually be carried out. If I call the crossing guard from a pay phone in another state, my threat to wrap the golf club around his neck will probably not be viewed seriously because I am not physically present to carry out the act. Furthermore, if I neglected to acquire a golf club to wrap around the neck of the crossing guard, then my threat would not be regarded seriously because I do not have the means with which to carry out my threat.

Unlike the tort of battery, the victim of an assault must be conscious of the threatened harm. If the in-tended victim is unaware of the threat, then it is impossible to commit an assault. If I raise a hefty leg of lamb over the head of the crossing guard while he is taking a nap at the crosswalk, then I cannot com-mit an assault because he is unaware that he might be in danger of suffering immediate harm to his phys-ical well-being. Assuming that I am determined to assault the crossing guard, I might tap him on the shoulder several times until he awakens and then hold the leg of lamb over his head in as menacing a manner as possible. When he realizes that I intend to strike him with a piece of meat that is not properly garnished, then he will probably feel the apprehension necessary to enable me to boast that I am a competent tortfeasor.

False imprisonment is a somewhat different intentional tort than battery or assault because it involves neither a harmful or offensive touching nor causing the victim to fear for his personal safety but instead relates to the deprivation of the liberty of the victim. In brief, false imprisonment consists of (1) an affirmative act by a wrongdoer (2) made with the intent to deprive the victim of his liberty (3) which results in actual confinement of the victim (4) so that the victim is either aware of his confinement or suffers actual injury from the confinement.

The wrongdoer need not personally supervise the confinement of the victim nor does the confinement itself have to be of a specified duration. I might believe that God has charged me with the task of imprisoning in the cavernous basement beneath my house every person who has ever worn nonmatching pairs of socks. Because I must personally round up these footwear heathens, I cannot stay behind to keep an eye on my prisoners so I would probably find it necessary to hire some security guards so that I could devote myself fully to getting these mismatchers off the streets. Even though I might not ever perform guard duty, I will be liable for holding my prisoners against their will because I was the mastermind who was responsible for their detention. Similarly, if my roundup is so successful that my basement becomes greatly overcrowded and I am forced to let people leave it within hours of their arrival so as to make room for the newest detainees, I will still be liable for false imprisonment even though the duration of confinement is not particularly significant.

A threat of force even in the absence of actual physical confinement will also constitute false imprisonment if that threat is sufficient to overcome the resistance of a reasonable person and cause her to remain against her will. If I leave all my detainees in a meadow (instead of a locked basement) in the middle of a city park and threaten to sic my attack armadillo on them should they try to escape, the detainees will not be forced to choose between staying behind and making a dash for freedom (and possibly being bitten by an armadillo). Less direct threats of harm other than the use of physical force may also be sufficient to constitute false imprisonment. If I threaten to expose the detainees' dirty little secret of sock incongruity to the world should they leave the meadow, then my threat might be regarded as sufficient to overcome the desire to leave of even the strongest-willed of my detainees. If my threat of exposure does in fact cause these people to remain in the meadow against their will, then I would still be liable for false imprisonment even though there are no physical barriers to prevent them from leaving. In cases that do not involve threats of physical violence, a finding of false imprisonment will depend on the nature of the threatened action as well as whether it was reasonable for the detainee to be intimidated enough to remain behind. Even if such a fear is not reasonable, my knowledge that a detainee is susceptible to a certain type of threat that would not intimidate an ordinary person, if used against that detainee, would probably render me liable for false imprisonment.

Liability for false imprisonment may also arise from a failure to release a person from confinement when that person is entitled to be released. If I run a youth camp that ostensibly teaches young campers survival techniques but also rents their labor services to local road paving companies, then my refusal to allow the campers to leave when the summer ends because I need some additional bodies to help pour asphalt for a nearby highway will cause me to be liable to my campers for false imprisonment. Even though I might point out that the eighty-hour workweeks on the roadbeds in the broiling sun have instilled discipline in my campers as well as caused many of them to have religious experiences, my conduct will not be excused.

Like the other intentional torts, the act of confinement by the wrongdoer must be accompanied by the intent on the part of the wrongdoer that the intended victim actually be deprived of his liberty. If an overly enthusiastic shopper loses track of the time and is locked in a department store after it closes through no fault of the store's employees, then neither the store manager nor her employees will be liable for false imprisonment because neither of them actually intended to confine the shopper. If the store manager made it a practice to lock the doors precisely at closing time regardless of whether all of the customers had actually left the premises, then the store manager might be liable for false imprisonment because there was a substantial certainty that some shoppers who had not yet spent all their worldly wealth were still inside.

False imprisonment may also arise in situations in which the wrongdoer fails to provide the detainee with a reasonable means of escape or fails to provide the assistance needed to make such an escape. If the demand for labor on highway projects evaporates so that I no longer have any reason to keep my campers in custody, my failure to unlock the gate to the camp so that the campers do not have to scramble over an electrified fence and dash through a mine field will cause me to be liable for false imprisonment because I failed to make available the only reasonable means of egress from the camp.

Even individuals such as police officers who have the authority to detain persons can be liable for false imprisonment if they use their authority in an improper manner. If a police officer arrests an individual for a criminal offense without a warrant, then he could be liable for improperly detaining the arrested individual if he made the arrest without having a reasonable belief that a felony had been committed and that the person he took into custody had committed the felony. A private individual making a citizen's arrest, by contrast, will be able to avoid liability for false imprisonment only if a felony has been committed and he has a reasonable basis for believing that the person he is holding has committed the crime. As far as misdemeanors are concerned, police officers and private citizens will not be liable for false imprisonment only if the warrantless arrest is made for a breach of the peace and it was committed in the immediate presence of the arresting party. A police officer who makes an arrest based on a warrant will not be liable for false imprisonment if he or she physically detains a person even if the warrant is later determined to be invalid.

The owner of a store may also be given a limited right to detain persons who he reasonably believes have shoplifted goods. The suspected shoplifter may not be detained for an unreasonable length of time nor may excessive force be used by the proprietor to detain the suspect. If Ed Cotton, the proprietor of Socks Unlimited, spots me stuffing a three-pack of argyles into my trousers and hauls me into the back room to hold me until the police arrive, he cannot use deadly force to prevent me from leaving the premises. Moreover, he cannot lock me in a closet for eight months to "soften me up" because such a period of time is vastly in excess of the time needed for him to conduct an investigation into my criminal proclivities. A court hearing my claim for false imprisonment would probably find that a few hours would have been more than sufficient for Ed Cotton to conduct his interrogation and retrieve the merchandise if he were so inclined.

The person claiming false imprisonment need not have suffered actual damages in order to sustain a claim, but he must either be aware of the confinement while he is being detained or have been injured during the confinement. If I followed Ed Cotton into the back room under the mistaken impression that I was to receive a prize for being the store's fifty thousandth customer, then my remaining there in the expectation that I would soon receive a complimentary package of woolens would prevent me from claiming that I had been unlawfully detained. After all, one cannot be deprived of one's liberty if one is not even aware that he is being held against his will.

The intentional infliction of emotional distress is the fourth and final of the intentional torts to the person that we shall discuss. As suggested by its title, this tort focuses on the deliberate infliction of emotional injuries and does not require a showing of physical damage. To be liable for the intentional infliction of emotional distress, the wrongdoer must (1) act in an outrageous and extreme manner (2) with the intent of causing severe emotional distress to the victim or with reckless disregard for the victim (3) which results in the victim suffering severe emotional distress. The absence of any requirement that there be a tangible physical injury necessitates that the act itself be shocking and far outside the bounds of acceptable behavior.

The acceptance of this tort has not been uniform because the absence of a tangible physical injury makes it nearly impossible to assess the damages suffered by the victim with any degree of certainty. Because it is difficult to determine whether a person's claim of injury due to shock is in fact genuine, the focus of this tort must turn to the behavior that allegedly caused the emotional distress. As a result, the plaintiff must prove that the defendant did in fact act in a manner that was so outrageous that it would shock the conscious of a person of ordinary sensibilities. If the party claiming the injury cannot demonstrate that the defendant acted in a manner that exceeds all limits of decency, then he or she will be unable to recover any damages for his or her injury.

The actual act that results in the infliction of emotional distress may range from outrageous business practices, such as making phone calls to threaten people with physical injury if they are slow in paying their bills, to abusing positions of authority, such as threatening to fire an employee for resisting unwanted sexual advances. In general, the use of bad language or colorful strings of naughty verbs will not be considered sufficient to meet the standards of this tort, perhaps because we have all become somewhat resigned to the common usage of such verbal manure. Yet if the intended victim is especially sensitive to noisy displays of such language and it appears that the wrongdoer knew of the intended victim's sensitivities and wanted to "shock" the victim, then the victim may be able to recover damages.

The intentional infliction of emotional distress often arises in situations in which there is some sort of special relationship such as that between an innkeeper and his guests or a mortician and a bereaved family using his services. If my great Uncle Buster finally goes to meet his Maker and I hire the Shady

Chapter 1

Tree Funeral Home and Specimen Market to prepare his remains for an open-casket memorial service, the fact that Uncle Buster appears at the service in an elegant ivory casket without his head (which was shipped by mistake to a medical school in Quebec) will probably cause many of my family members to scream uncontrollably thus shattering the solemn dignity of the occasion. More than a few mourners may have recurring dreams of a headless Uncle Buster riding through the countryside on a black steed, but several of my relatives will be practical enough to consult their phone directory for the nearest attorney. The mishandling of corpses arguably provides one of the best opportunities for recovering for the intentional infliction of emotional distress.

The absence of a physical injury requirement muddies any attempt to demonstrate a causal relationship between the wrongdoer's conduct and the emotional injury suffered by the victim. The ability to demonstrate a causal relationship is further complicated when the wrongdoer intentionally causes physical injury to one person but another party claims to have suffered emotional injury. The person claiming the emotional injury must demonstrate that he was present when the wrongdoer inflicted the physical injury and that he was a close relation of the party who suffered the physical injury. The claimant may also have to prove that the wrongdoer knew that the claimant was both physically present and related to the party who suffered the physical injury.

As far as the damages that need to be proven are concerned, the absence of a physical injury requirement necessitates that the injured party demonstrate that she has suffered severe emotional distress. Proof of the same might include certain physical symptoms (such as weight loss, increased blood pressure, and loss of appetite) that would indicate that the normal physiological functions had been disrupted by emotional trauma. Such symptoms could be subject to differing interpretations so it is likely that a calculation of damages would ultimately rest on the outrageousness of the defendant's conduct as well as the emotional distress suffered by the claimant.

Intentional Torts to Property

There are a number of intentional torts that interfere with the property rights of others including trespass to land, trespass to chattels (personal property), and conversion which are available to those persons who would like to commit a tort but believe themselves to be too refined to commit an intentional tort against the person of another. Any one of these torts will leave the would-be tortfeasor with that warm, glowing feeling that professional wrongdoers often feel after committing more "glamorous" torts such as assault and battery. For the novice wrongdoer, there is no better tort to commit than that of trespass to land because it is usually quite easy to find real property owned by another on which to trespass.

Although its title is somewhat self-explanatory, a trespass to land consists of (1) an intentional act by the wrongdoer (2) that interferes with the owner's possessory interest (3) in real property. Fortunately for those persons who abhor walking or otherwise exercising their legs, it is not necessary to enter the land to commit a trespass. One can invade another person's possessory interest in land by flooding the land or dumping trash on the property or even throwing a rock across the property line. If I am the proprietor of a company that generates significant amounts of hazardous waste and I hit upon the idea of disposing of that waste by tossing it onto my neighbor's property, then I will have committed a trespass to that property even though neither I nor any of my employees ever physically set foot on that property. It would also be possible for me to commit a trespass if I was invited onto that land by the owner but I refused to leave the premises after we concluded our meeting. Because my company would no longer be desired by the owner, my continued presence would interfere with his possessory interest in his property.

One can commit a trespass beneath or above the surface of the land of another. If I tunnel underneath the adjoining property in search of the lost city of the gnomes with its fabled fountain of lard, my subterranean incursion will still be regarded as a trespass even though the neighboring property owner has no interest in gnomes or the mythology of the fountain of lard and would never consider digging any deeper than his basement floor. My interference with his possessory interest in the property would still constitute a trespass even though he has no plans to make any use of that portion of his property. Less clear is how far down into the earth my neighbor's possessory interest extends because it will lose all practical meaning at subterranean depths that cannot be reached using existing technology. A more useful approach might be to argue that I cannot interfere with my neighbor's useable subsurface property rights or do anything beneath the surface of his property that otherwise interferes with his activities on the surface. If my incessant burrowing in search of the fountain of lard causes my neighbor's house to disappear into a giant pit, then I will have interfered with his useable property rights as well as incurred the costs of rebuilding his home.

The same principle of useable property rights applies to the area above the surface of my neighbor's property. To what height must he have free and unfettered use of the atmosphere above his land? The height to which he can throw a rock? The top of his roof? Because we live in an age of air travel in which airplanes are constantly flying over private property, permitting individual landowners to claim that they have exclusive rights above their property all the way up to the sky would be absurd because it would make air and space travel legally impossible. The typical cross-country plane flight would have to obtain tens of thousands of permissions from the landowners beneath its flight path before it could leave the ground. Consequently, it is more reasonable to focus on the activities that the landowner could reasonably be expected to engage in on his property and determine how high his possessory interests above the surface of the property should extend so that he may make full use of the land. Because we do not want to impede air travel unnecessarily, the typical suburban homeowner's possessory interest above the surface of his property would probably be limited to a few hundred feet. This standard would be less stringent in urban environments having many tall buildings.

What if my next-door neighbor takes up rocketry as a hobby and begins building twenty-foot tall missiles that can be shot thirty miles up into the atmosphere? Because he has the need for a much higher "ceiling" than his less flamboyant neighbors who busy themselves with such mundane activities as golf, tennis, and burrowing, it would appear that he could claim a correspondingly higher "tube" of property rights into the atmosphere because he could shoot down passing planes or blimps. Unfortunately, the legal authorities would tell him that he did not have the right to shoot down airplanes and that his useable property rights extended no higher than those of his neighbors. He would probably also be threatened with a jail term of several centuries if he continued to pursue his hobby. In short, the planes crossing overhead will not be found to have interfered with my neighbor's property rights because he does not need to exclude them from his airspace to make reasonable use of his land.

The trespasser need not intend to cause any of the consequences that result from interfering with the possessory interests of the landowner; he needs only to intend to commit the trespass itself. Unlike the intentional torts such as assault and battery in which the wrongdoer commits an act with the intent of bringing about a desired result, a wrongdoer needs only to intend to trespass in order for the requisite intent to be found. Any mistakes regarding the ownership of the land will not provide a defense to the trespass if the trespasser intended to go onto the land. On the other hand, my inadvertent entry onto the property of another resulting from my losing control of my bicycle and careening off the road into the front yard of my next-door neighbor would not be a trespass because I did not intend to go onto his property.

Once a trespass is found, damages will be presumed to exist. The actual calculation of the damages to be awarded to the landowner (assuming that he, and not a lessee, for example, is the party entitled to possession) will depend on the physical damage caused to the property by the trespasser. If I am a trespasser who likes to commit my specialty on the cheap by tiptoeing onto other properties to minimize the amount of damage caused by my unauthorized intrusions, I will still be liable for some nominal amount even if I do not cause any ascertainable damages. On the other hand, the serious trespasser who reads Nietzsche and believes in scorched-earth intrusions such as sweeping the trespassed area with a flamethrower will be liable not only for damages resulting from the trespass itself, such as broken fences and damaged trees, but also for any foreseeable or unforeseeable consequences of her trespass such as the property damage resulting from her fires.

The consent of the party entitled to possession of the property will act as a complete defense to a trespass. However, the consent must be given by the party actually entitled to possession of the property. If the owner consents to the trespass but had previously leased the land to a tenant who did not consent to the trespass, then the intruder will still be liable for trespassing because he did not obtain permission from the party legally entitled to possession of the property.

A person may also enter the property of another to reclaim his own personal property. If my pet armadillo wanders onto my next-door neighbor's land, I am entitled to cross over onto his property to reclaim my beast. If at all possible, I must seek the permission of my neighbor before entering his land unless it is patently obvious that such a request would be futile (as would be the case if my neighbor had died the night before). However, this right of entry is limited so that although I will not be liable for trespass, I will be strictly liable (regardless of intent) for any damages that I cause to the land while chasing after my fleeing animal. In short, I would have to pay for the privilege of tromping through my neighbor's vegetable garden and knocking down his clothesline. If my neighbor had stolen my armadillo, then my privilege to enter his land to reclaim my property would be somewhat greater in scope as I would not be liable for any damages done to the vegetable garden or the clothesline so long as those damages were incurred while I was trying to recover my pet.

An unauthorized entry onto the land of another will be excused if the entry by the would-be trespasser is made to prevent or somehow mitigate a disaster so long as the conduct is reasonable under the circumstances. If a thunderstorm begins while I am floating on my inflatable rubber duck in the middle of a lake, then my paddling through the raging currents and howling winds to the nearest shore will be considered reasonable conduct even though I make my landing on the property of another. The damage caused by my landing on the shore is insignificant, whereas the result avoided by the landing (my untimely death) is relatively important. As a result, it is unlikely that I would be liable for trespassing. Of course this outcome presupposes that I continue to behave myself while on the property. If I am particularly ebullient after having avoided my close brush with death and I dash through the landowner's house screaming with joy and interrupt a wedding service being held there by knocking over the top tier of the cake, then I will be responsible for those damages because my actions cannot be considered reasonable since I am no longer in any mortal danger from the storm.

The right of entry based on necessity as described above must be contrasted with the right to enter the property of another to abate a nuisance. If my neighbor decides to raise the ante after having tired of my incessant burrowing beneath his land and begins manufacturing an extremely concentrated form of the repulsively flowery perfume favored by my Aunt Agatha (which causes dizziness and fainting spells), then I might have no choice but to go into his land and blow up his perfume vat. My privilege to enter his land to rid myself of this nuisance will necessarily depend on my demonstrating that the perfume was so pungent and had so pervaded my land that it was virtually impossible for me to enjoy the use of my property.

Before I could enter my neighbor's land to eliminate the nuisance, I would have to have requested and been denied permission to enter the property. I would also have to demonstrate the aforementioned interference with my property rights and that I had made reasonable efforts prior to my entry onto my neighbor's property to reduce the effects of the nuisance on my land. Because we are talking about a pervasive odor, it is unclear if anything short of a very tall boundary wall or the installation of a row of massive fans to blow the odor back onto my neighbor's land could deal adequately with the problem. Such measures would not be reasonable owing to their excessive costs and technical shortcomings so I would probably not have to concern myself greatly with making significant ameliorative efforts. I would also have to show that my destruction of the nuisance was not unlawful and that I did not breach the peace or cause any injuries to any persons. That would be a rather tall order if I destroyed the perfume vat with a box of dynamite. On the other hand, I might be able to rewire the perfume vat so that it no longer cooked its precious liquid in such a malodorous fashion thus reducing its pollution of my property.

The personal property counterpart to a trespass to land is a trespass to chattels, which consists of (1) an intentional act by the wrongdoer (2) that interferes with the injured party's possessory rights (3) in personal property (4) and that results in damages to the personal property. It is essentially the same tort as a trespass to land, but it involves personal property instead of realty. A trespass to chattels may consist of any interference with the possessory rights of another party. This interference may range from an intermeddling that involves the unauthorized use of the property without the intent to claim any rights of ownership in the property to a dispossession in which the wrongdoer asserts a claim of ownership in the property against the person entitled to possession.

The act resulting in the trespass must be accompanied by the intent on the part of the trespasser to do the act that results in the trespass. If I knowingly take a crystal salt shaker from my table at La Sadomie (one of the more highly regarded French restaurants in my town) and then saunter out of the room with the salt shaker in my pocket, I will have committed a trespass because my actions interfered with the restaurant's possessory interest in the salt shaker. Whether my offense can be characterized as a dispossession or an intermeddling will depend on whether I planned to assert any rights of ownership in the salt shaker against the restaurant. If I took the salt shaker so that I might sprinkle the lobby of the restaurant with salt to celebrate the beginning of the Year of the Slug, then my trespass would be considered an intermeddling because I intended to bring the salt shaker back to the table after completing my religious ritual. If I took the salt shaker home because I mistakenly believed that it was the same salt shaker I had lost while scampering along a nude beach on the French Riviera, then my action would be construed as a claim of ownership in the restaurant's salt shaker and regarded as a dispossession. The fact that I did not intend to commit a trespass is irrelevant; it is my intent to commit the act (taking the salt shaker) that interferes with the possessory rights of the owner and renders me liable for trespass. I would still be liable even if I mistakenly believed that it was legal to take salt shakers out of French restaurants because ignorance of the law will not excuse liability when the trespassory act itself is intentionally committed.

The characterization of a trespass as a dispossession or as intermeddling will also determine the measure of damages awarded. A dispossession will entail liability for any damages to the salt shaker as well as the value of the salt shaker that was lost while it was in my possession. An intermeddling will result in an award of damages only if there is some actual damage to the salt shaker as would be the case if I accidentally flung it through the lobby window while performing a particularly strenuous religious exercise to celebrate the passing of the Year of the Locust.

As with the other intentional torts, the consent of the owner to the defendant's use of the property will serve as a complete defense to a charge of trespass. One could also use any of the defenses to assault and battery for defeating liability for trespass under the appropriate circumstances. As a result, the consent of the proprietor of La Sodomie to my taking the salt shaker home overnight will bar any subsequent attempts by him to have me charged with a trespass. He will also not be privileged to enter my home and reclaim the property without my consent because he agreed that I could take the salt shaker.

The difference between a trespass to chattels and a conversion is largely one of degree; the tort of conversion deals with situations in which the trespass is so extreme or the damage to the personal property so great that the wrongdoer should be required to pay the full value of the damaged property. Consequently, there is no clear-cut distinction between a trespass to chattels and conversion; one shades into the other depending on the extent of the damages sought to be recovered.

For those who find the tort of trespass to chattels to be too tame, conversion may be just the thing for putting the thrill back into one's daily affairs. Converters of property rank higher than trespassers to land and chattels in the eyes of most self-respecting tortfeasors because the actions of the former amount to outright claims of ownership against the rightful owners instead of mere interferences with their possession. A conversion consists of (1) an act by the wrongdoer (2) done with the intent of asserting exclusive control over personal property (3) owned by another person (4) that causes substantial damages to the property.

The actual act depriving the owner of her property may take on a variety of forms. One can destroy the personal property or significantly alter it. Consequently, my driving my Aunt Agatha's 1932 Rolls Royce into a tree while trying to run down a snake crawling across the road could render me liable for conversion if my act was accompanied by the intent to destroy her property. The result would be the same if I smashed her Rolls Royce into a massive stone wall as part of my study of the structural integrity of classic motorcars if I did the act with the intent of destroying Aunt Agatha's property. Even though my study might have great appeal to automobile nihilists and anarchists, my destruction of the property would be considered tantamount to an assertion of ownership contrary to the rights of Aunt Agatha. Similarly, if I take a blowtorch to Aunt Agatha's motorcar with the thought of resculpting the body to give it a more contemporary look, then my amateur styling efforts will be considered a substantial alteration of the motorcar and thus a conversion.

A conversion may also be committed if one uses the property of another without permission or sells the property to a third party without the permission of the owner. Using Aunt Agatha's Roll Royce as a battering ram will cause me to be liable for conversion because my use was not authorized by Aunt Agatha and resulted in substantial damages to her property. Although some well-timed whimpering and groveling at Aunt Agatha's feet might cause her to forgive me for my behavioral shortcomings, I would still be liable for any damages to the property. The same would be true if I needed some extra pocket money and sold Aunt Agatha's Rolls Royce to a wandering band of elves who were in need of a fancy motorcar for the fairyland ball. Even though my sale of Aunt Agatha's property might have been prompted by the heartfelt pleas of the elves (who wished to avoid the ridicule that would invariably result if they showed up at the ball on foot) as well as my less laudable selfish desires to increase my own wealth at the expense of my wealthy relative, I would be liable for the full replacement value of the motorcar because my sale of the same was not authorized by Aunt Agatha.

Because the tort of conversion focuses on the un-authorized use of property or the actual injury to property owned by another, my failure to return the motorcar to Aunt Agatha after she requests the same will also constitute an unwarranted interference with her property assuming that I have no right to main-tain continued possession of the motorcar. If I had leased the motorcar from Aunt Agatha for one month and she began to have second thoughts two weeks later when she saw me pick up an entry form at the local automobile club for a demolition derby, she would not be able to demand the return of her property until the expiration of the one-month period unless I ac-tually did intend to drive her motorcar in the derby. The use of her motorcar in a demolition derby was probably not contemplated by Aunt Agatha when she signed the lease so she would be within her rights to demand its return if I showed up at the track in her motorcar wearing my crash helmet ready to do battle with two dozen other cars lacking assorted doors, trunks, roofs, etc. Consequently, conversion may be found if one treats the property of another in a man-ner that is beyond the scope of its authorized use.

As with the other intentional torts, the act result-ing in interference with the possessory interests of the owner must be accompanied by the intent to effect the same. If I suffer an anxiety attack and run Aunt Agatha's motorcar into a truck or accidentally cut off the back third of the chasis while testing out my new chain saw, my act would not be considered conversion because I lacked the intent to damage the motorcar. Even if I was careless in my handling of the motorcar while navigating the highways of my town or in wielding my chainsaw, I would not be considered a converter because my actions were not sufficiently purposeful or deliberate.

Conversion may be viewed as a more serious version of the tort of trespass to chattels so an action based on conversion may be sustained only if the damage to the property is significant. My getting fingerprints on the steering wheel of Aunt Agatha's motorcar will not be considered significant enough to justify an action for conversion because my fingerprints alone do not cause tangible injury to the property. Even if Aunt Agatha is compulsively immaculate and goes so far as to send her maid's cleaning rags to the laundry, her belief that I have soiled the motorcar and thus caused its value to plummet will not be taken seriously because a court will calculate the damages based on an objective standard. Consequently, I may run my fingers all over the steering wheel with glee and not lose any sleep over the thought that I might be dragged into court for conversion.

Because conversion is regarded as a diabolical offense by all right-thinking property owners, the remedy for a finding of conversion may be a forced purchase of the converted property. Because the defendant has seriously damaged or interfered with property owned by another, the courts will often order that the wrongdoer be required to pay for the converted property. In effect, the converter will be forced to purchase the property that he has wrongfully treated as his own by his conduct. This is not to say that a court might not order the payment of damages for less than the full value of the converted property but such a remedy would probably be used only where the property had not been so severely damaged as to justify the payment of the replacement value. Even though we might long for the days of Merrie Olde England where those who committed property crimes were often hung, today's converter would likely face only one of two comparatively mild remedies: the forced purchase of the converted property or some lesser amount of damages. The fact that the converter might be able to return the personal property in its original state would not bar the application of these remedies because the converter presumably interfered with the property in such a manner as to justify the imposition of either one of these two remedies. However, the converter can raise any of the defenses that could be used to defeat liability for a trespass to chattels to avoid such penalties.

CHAPTER 2

Defamation and Privacy

---

*Blind mouths! that scarce
themselves know how to
hold a sheep hook.*

— John Milton

2

Defamation

Defamation is sometimes regarded as a close relation of the intentional torts discussed in the previous chapter because it consists of activities that have no utility to society. Although a linguistics professor might argue that one person's description of how a prominent businessman spent the night with a quarterhorse is simply a colorful verbal nugget that enriches our language, the person whose reputation was smeared by such a tale would not find the story to be of great value. It is more likely that the defamed businessman would want to punish the person who spread the vile rumor or at least sell the movie rights to the highest bidder. In any event, most people would agree that some safeguards are needed to prevent individuals from arbitrarily damaging the reputations of others without fear of legal consequences.

Defamation includes those activities such as name-calling and outright lies that civilized persons such as ourselves like to engage in when we become bored with life and want to do something rotten without physically harming anybody. Given the proliferation of gossipy magazines and television shows, it is now possible to destroy another person's reputation in the blink of an eye. The speed with which a defamatory statement can be transmitted around the country has made it even more crucial that the legal rights of defamed persons be safeguarded. However, it is not always easy for a person to prove that she was defamed by a particular statement.

A defamatory statement may be oral (slander) or written (libel). A statement will be regarded as libel if it is recorded or otherwise reproduced in any permanent form. The publication in a newspaper, for example, of my defamatory statement about William Dullard, a local politician, being a thief and a liar will be categorized as libel because it is reproduced in written form. Similarly, a record or tape of my unflattering statement about William Dullard could be characterized as libel because it was recorded in a permanent form that may be reproduced and disseminated to a wide audience. Although this statement might not be of great interest to political scientists, it would stir some interest at the local news stations because Dullard would likely criticize my statement as being little more than a cheap shot.

Although most people would be hard-pressed to describe the elements that must be proven in order to sustain an action for defamation, common sense tells us that the statement must somehow devalue the reputation of the person being defamed. Although anyone may utter or write a defamatory statement, the prospective plaintiff will have to demonstrate (1) that the defendant intentionally made a defamatory statement (2) about the plaintiff (3) that was published by the defendant to a third party (4) resulting in damages to the plaintiff's reputation. Although the creativity of the defamatory statement is limited only by the defendant's ability to string together colorful nouns and verbs, the defamatory statement itself must somehow impair the plaintiff's reputation. If I call you an unprincipled molester of armadillos in an ancient Babylonian dialect that only a handful of dusty historians can understand, then my statement might not be considered defamatory if disseminated to the general population because no one would understand what it meant. Consequently, you could not claim that your reputation had been damaged. The result would be different, however, if a translation of my remarks accompanied its transmission so that everybody understood what I had said and now made armadillo noises when passing you on the street.

A statement is defamatory on its face if the listener does not need any additional information to understand the nature of the defamatory remark or identify the defamed party. However, a statement may be defamatory even if its content does not directly impugn the reputation of the plaintiff so long as its defamatory nature can be revealed by reference to extrinsic facts. If I publish a report congratulating Ann Gland for her recent delivery of her ninth child, my statement may be found to be defamatory if Ann proves that she is actually a chaste nun. Once these extrinsic facts become apparent, Ann will be able to argue that I have defamed her and that her reputation has been damaged.

An alternative standard for determining whether a statement is defamatory focuses on whether its contents would expose the plaintiff to "public hatred, contempt, or ridicule." Although such a standard might make it difficult to defame a professor of Marxism owing to the beleaguered state of that discipline, it does provide another yardstick for measuring the extent to which a defamatory statement has lowered the esteem in which the community holds the plaintiff. However, there are situations in which one might be subject to ridicule but not suffer damages to one's reputation. The publication of an erroneous report announcing my being ordained as a priest when I am actually the somewhat sleazy owner of the Erotic Kingdom, a massive supermarket of bawdy books, movies, and novelties would be one such example. Because my reputation is already lower than that of the used car salesman who peddles his inventory on late-night television, it is difficult to see how my reputation could be harmed by the report even though some of my acquaintances might poke fun at my "career change."

One may defame a deceased individual but the representatives of the deceased individual's estate will not be permitted to maintain an action for defamation. Only individuals who are living may pursue a claim for defamation; deceased individuals cannot suffer from any damage to their reputation caused by a defamatory remark. If I call my Aunt Agatha a penny-pinching bag of bones, then she can pursue her defamation claim against me because she is still around to suffer personally the damage caused to her reputation by my remark. On the other hand, I can call my deceased Uncle Buster (whose head recently turned up in a hatter's display window in Iceland) a thief and a liar because he is dead and his legal representatives have no right to sue me for defamation. Even if I stood near his grave and made disparaging remarks about Uncle Buster's lifelong study of horned toads, a species whose ancestors he believed had built the Pyramids and invented four-color magazine advertising, I still could not be sued for defamation. This is not to say that I could not be forcibly ejected from the cemetery for trespassing or perhaps for being a nuisance, but my freedom to denounce my deceased uncle would not be silenced by a court of law.

The law of defamation focuses on the extent to which a person's reputation has been damaged. It does not encompass jokes that are made at the expense of a person because it is unlikely that people will think less of a person who is the butt of a few jokes. However, this standard may not be absolute because a particularly mean-spirited joke calculated to damage the reputation of its victim could be considered defamatory if it would cause a reasonable person to think less of the victim. This standard of offensiveness would admittedly be difficult to attain given the freedom with which most comedians are able to comment about other people, particularly public figures.

Chapter 2

Because we are concerned with what the community itself considers to be defamatory, a statement may not be considered as such if it is offensive to only a very tiny portion of the population. If you describe the leader of a local religious cult as a charlatan because he believes that the universe was created by a mystical three-humped camel, he might argue that your statement was blasphemous and defamatory. Yet if nobody else in the community raises an eyebrow at your comments, then the leader may not be able to demonstrate that you made a defamatory remark because the community itself does not consider it to be sufficiently offensive. The same reasoning would apply if you made a similar comment about the cult itself because it is possible to defame organizations as well as individuals.

A plaintiff must also show that the defamatory statement actually relates to him in order for him to bring an action against the speaker. I cannot sue you for calling Aunt Agatha a feeble-minded fool because your statement did not damage my reputation. The right to sue for defamation is personal to the party who was the focus of the defamatory statement. Aunt Agatha would have to demonstrate that a reasonable person hearing your nasty remark about her biting the heads off rodents would know that she was the individual to whom you were referring.

A somewhat different situation arises when one makes a defamatory remark about an entire group of people, such as the members of an organization. If I say that the people who work for Weasel Motors, a major automobile producer, are unprincipled, money-

grubbing, woodenheaded fascists, a company employee's right to sue me for defamation will depend
on whether my statement refers to some or all of the
employees, the size of the group about which I am
speaking, and whether there are any particular facts
that would enable that employee to show that she
had been singled out by my statement. The larger
the group, the less likely it is that a member of that
group will be able to demonstrate that my defamatory remarks directly relate to her. A contrary conclusion would result if I referred explicitly to the
security guard who sits next to the elevators on the
fifth floor of the company's corporate headquarters
because my listeners would be able to identify the
person about whom I was speaking. As the members
of the defamed group became more numerous, however, it would become increasingly difficult for any
one of them to prove that a statement actually defamed a particular member. One would be relatively
safe calling all lawyers quibbling pettifoggers or all
doctors ignorant empirics, but the risk of liability
would grow correspondingly greater as the size of the
group diminished. If I declare that most of the thirty
women in the local gardening club are prostitutes,
then those members who consider my remarks to be
defamatory might be able to demonstrate that their
individual reputations have been damaged owing to
the small size of the group. If my fellow townspeople
ranked prostitutes above doctors and lawyers in pres-
tige and considered gardening devotees to be little
more than human vermin, then a different result
might occur. In such a situation, my calling a gar-

dening club member a prostitute might be considered a great compliment so that it would be impossible to damage the reputations of the club members by such a statement.

A defamatory statement must be published before one can maintain an action for defamation. This publication requirement does not mean that the statement must appear in print but only that it must be communicated to and understood by a third party. If you run around town calling me a dirty skunk in a language that sounds like porcine grunts, then the publication requirement will not be met because it is extremely unlikely that anyone who heard you would know what you were saying. If a linguistics professor happened to pass by you on his bicycle while you were filling the air with grunts and was able to decipher your message, then the publication requirement would be satisfied.

Whether the party publishing the defamatory communication believes it to be defamatory is not relevant because it is the intent to publish—not the intent to defame—that must exist to satisfy the publication requirement. If I tell my Aunt Agatha that you are an egg snatcher knowing that she has a pathological hatred of people who steal dairy products, it is my intent to pass this information on to Aunt Agatha and not the content of the communication itself that constitutes publication. However, there can be no publication if you boast to Aunt Agatha that you steal all types of eggs under cover of darkness before I am able to communicate the same information to her. If I decide to write a book to tell the world about your hankering for eggs and the book becomes a best-seller, you might decide to sue the bookstores and libraries that carry this book for defamation to get it pulled off the shelves. These so-called secondary publishers of the allegedly defamatory work will not be liable for defamation if they had no knowledge that it was defamatory.

Publishers are also protected by the single publication rule, which requires that all the copies of a defamatory book or newspaper article be treated as a single publication even though the damages arising from the distribution of the defamatory material will be calculated based upon the story's effect on the total readership. Any entity that is involved in the initial transmission of the defamatory material (regardless of whether it is a newspaper, book publisher, radio station, or television station) will be treated as a primary publisher and will be held to the same standard of liability as the person who made the defamatory statement. Consequently, the publisher of my book about your egg-snatching adventures will incur the same liability for defamation as I will because my publisher is responsible for the initial distribution of my defamatory book. If you sell the book's paperback rights to another publisher who brings out a softcover version of my dairy product thriller six months after the book is first published, the paperback publisher will incur the same liability as the original publisher. Whether the paperback publisher actually believes that the book is true is irrelevant because it intended to publish the book.

Chapter 2

The would-be plaintiff must also demonstrate that the publication of the defamatory statement has caused her to suffer damages. Special damages are those financial or monetary losses suffered by the plaintiff that result from the publication of the defamatory statement. Special damages might include the loss of a job or an inheritance as well as the loss of a contract or a gift. Special damages must have some monetary value. Such things as the humiliation or aggravation caused by the defamatory statement will not be included in a calculation of special damages because such items are more emotional than financial in nature. Liability on the part of the defendant for special damages will be found only if these damages result from the reactions of third parties to the defamatory statement. If a prospective employer refuses to hire you after reading my account of how you pinched an egg from a supermarket, then you could claim that you had suffered special damages from my defamatory statement because it arguably cost you a job. On the other hand, no special damages would be found if the prospective employer had actually been in the supermarket on the day you were rummaging through the dairy case and saw you stuff an egg in your pocket because he would have learned about your egg-poaching habit through personal observation and not my book. Consequently, he would have obtained first-hand knowledge of your behavior so that his reaction could not be prompted by his subsequent review of my book.

There are several exceptions to the requirement that special damages to the plaintiff's reputation must be shown before an action for defamation can proceed. If a slanderous (oral) statement falls within one of four particular categories, it will be characterized as slander per se and damages will be presumed to exist under the law. First, defamatory statements regarding a person's qualifications for her particular trade or profession or her conduct of the same will be presumed to cause pecuniary damages. However, the defamatory remark must impugn some aspect of the plaintiff's occupation that is relevant to the competent performance of her job duties. If I call a lawyer a liar, then my statement will be regarded as defamatory because a lawyer's reputation for honesty is crucial to her ability to attract clients and thus make a living. If I call a burglar a liar, then damages will not necessarily be presumed because it is difficult to see how such an accusation would impair the ability of the burglar to make a living. Similarly, my statement that the neighborhood grocer cannot speak French would not adversely affect his ability to make a living and thus would not constitute slander per se; a different outcome might result if I announced that a professor of French at the local college could not speak the language. In the latter case, my statement would amount to an accusation that the professor was incompetent. This statement could damage his professional reputation as well as hinder his ability to obtain a job elsewhere.

Second, a statement that a person has committed a crime involving moral turpitude will be slanderous per se and will not require proof of special damages. Crimes of moral turpitude include such things as fondling sheep, exposing oneself to crossing guards, and any other type of illegal behavior having immoral or carnal aspects. Although our tolerance for such unseemly behavior seems to have grown as our sense of morality has rotted, such accusations do not usually bolster one's reputation. If I accuse you of sleeping with a minor named Dominique Thunderbolt, then my statement would be slanderous per se because I would be claiming that you had committed statutory rape. The fact that I may believe myself to be performing a public service by writing a book about the incident and selling the graphic photographs to a tabloid is not the issue because I did intend to make the defamatory remark. Such an accusation will be considered defamatory on its face, and you will not have to prove that you have suffered special damages.

Third, a declaration that a person has a horrible disease will excuse the plaintiff from having to prove pecuinary damages. This category has generally been limited to diseases such as venereal disease and leprosy so that my statement about you having freckles or very bad breath will not reach the "loathsomeness" threshold needed to constitute slander per se. Similarly, I cannot declare that you have "leprosy *and* a brilliant smile" and thereby escape liability. My attempt to water down the defamatory statement to avoid having the statement characterized as slander per se while conveying the gist of the message will not be tolerated.

Finally, a statement that impugns the chastity of a woman will not require proof of special damages. If Dominique Thunderbolt's continued insistence on wearing her bunny slippers to bed finally causes you to lose your temper and call her an unflattering name that implies she hops from bed to bed, then Dominique would not have to prove special damages to maintain an action for defamation. Whether this particular category will continue to constitute slander per se in the future owing to our changing standards of morality is not clear. For the time being, however, it is best to be tolerant of bunny slippers and flannel nightwear.

We noted previously that slander consists of defamatory oral statements, whereas libel consists of defamatory remarks that are recorded in some permanent form such as print or electromagnetic tape. Because the more enduring nature of libel makes it possible for the defamatory remark to be repeated or otherwise disseminated without limit, the requirement that special damages be proven is often waived when dealing with libel. However, many states distinguish between a statement that is *libel on its face* and a statement that is *libel per quod*. The former term includes defamatory statements that require no knowledge of any additional facts to understand the defamatory message. The latter term refers to defamatory statements that require that reference be made to extrinsic information to understand the defamatory message. If I write a newspaper column characterizing you as an unclean, perverted agnostic, most readers would be able to understand the unflattering message contained in the column without knowing anything about you. Consequently, such a statement would be libel on its face. However, if I announced in my column that you would soon be leaving for Brazil to marry your long-time companion, such a statement might be characterized as libel per quod if additional information revealed that you were already married to another person. Proof of special damages will usually be required for statements that are libel per quod unless the content of the message falls within one of the traditional slander per se categories discussed above.

Whether the defamed person is a public official or public figure as opposed to a private person will determine the degree of care that the defendant must exercise before deciding to publish potentially defamatory information. It is much more difficult for a public official or public figure to recover damages for defamatory statements than it is for private individuals because the former must demonstrate that the defendant was reckless in its decision to publish the statement, whereas the latter needs only to show that the decision to publish was made negligently. Yet before we discuss the different standards for public figures and private citizens, we need to differentiate between the two categories of individuals.

Public figures are those persons who have achieved such widespread fame or notoriety that they enjoy extraordinary prominence in society. Movie stars, athletes, and other celebrities would be considered public figures. This is not an occupational definition, however, because an obscure actor who performs the operas of Richard Wagner on a streetcorner will not be considered a public figure for purposes of defamation. An actor might need to have starred on the stage or screen and perhaps have been divorced half a dozen times to be considered a public figure. Regardless of the occupation, we would expect a public figure's name to be recognized by a significant percentage of the people on the street.

Public figures might also be otherwise unknown individuals who voluntarily inject themselves into a matter of great public controversy. If my incompetent gardener, Otto Hertz, strongly believes that the vulture should replace the eagle as the national symbol and his views initiate a vigorous national debate in which he is a highly visible participant, then Otto will be considered a public figure as far as it relates to his participation in this particular controversy. He will be regarded as a private citizen for all other purposes. Otto will have to prove that a defamatory report about his crusade to replace the national symbol was made with *malice* in order to recover damages; he would only have to prove negligence if he was reported to be romantically involved with a starlet because Otto's womanizing is not the reason for which he attained public prominence.

Those persons who make statements allegedly defaming public figures enjoy a qualified privilege to publish such statements. A public figure seeking to recover damages will have to prove that the statement was made with the knowledge that it was false or that it was made with a reckless disregard for the truth. This finding of malice provides the constitutional threshold that must be met in order to defeat this qualified privilege. If I declare that the well-known singer Wanda Warbler (whose voice

has been favorably compared to the sound a fin-
gernail makes when it scratches a chalkboard) lip-
syncs all of her concert performances without bothering to verify the truth of this statement, then my
statement will not be privileged because it was made
with a reckless disregard for the truth. The same
outcome will result if I had made the statement
knowing that Wanda Warbler always sings live at
her concerts.

Like public figures, public officials must demonstrate that a defamatory statement was made with
malice. The term *public officials* includes elected pol-
iticians as well as candidates for elective office and
prominent political appointees. Yet one does not need
to be associated with the national government to be
considered a public official. The mayor of a town would
be considered a public official because she is well-
known locally and enjoys certain significant decision-
making powers. A report in the local newspaper that
the mayor takes bribes only when she really needs
the money would be considered defamatory; the mayor
would have to demonstrate that the statement was
made with knowledge of its falsity or with a reckless
disregard for the truth. Because the allegation that
the mayor takes bribes does adversely affect her
professional reputation, that statement will enjoy a
qualified privilege that may be defeated only if the
mayor can prove malice. The scope of this privilege
is necessarily limited to those matters relating to the
mayor's performance of her job; the mayor will not
have to prove malice if the defamatory remark relates to more private matters such as the mayor's

habit of pulling the wings off houseflies and watching them stumble around.

Private individuals who are involuntarily thrust into the spotlight owing to their being parties in a highly publicized lawsuit, for example, will not have to prove malice to recover damages. A private citizen will only need to show that the defendant was negligent in permitting the defamatory statement to be published. The negligence requirement could be satisfied by showing that a newspaper reporter, for example, failed to verify the accuracy of a quote attributed to the plaintiff by a third party. It is a much more difficult task to show malice because the plaintiff would have to prove that the defendant knew that the statement was false or that the defendant had grave doubts about the statement's validity when the decision to publish was made. However, the failure of the private citizen to prove malice will limit his recovery from the defendant to pecuniary damages. Consequently, there will be no award based on the presumption that the plaintiff has been defamed as would be the case if malice could be shown.

As with the intentional torts, the defendant can avail herself of several defenses to avoid liability for defamation. If the defendant obtained the plaintiff's permission to publish statements that would otherwise be defamatory, then the defendant will not incur liability for defamation. If I give you permission to print an article about some of the techniques I used to defraud a commercial lender, then I cannot argue that I was defamed because my consent would suggest that I did not believe my reputation would be damaged by the article. If I do not believe that I have been damaged, then I would have no reason to pursue a claim for defamation.

If a defamatory statement is true, then the defendant will be protected from any liability for libel or slander. Truth is an absolute defense and will generally defeat liability for defamation. However, the statement must·be accurate and must not be so ambiguous that it could lead to differing interpretations. If I report that my gardener, Otto Hertz, used to be a member of the secret police, a reader would probably understand that statement to mean that Otto used to be involved in an internal security force that used terror tactics to bully innocent people. The article would not be completely accurate if it neglected to explain that Otto was a member of an undercover gardening police detail at the local botanical garden whose job was to keep young children from stepping on the grass and elderly ladies from picking blooms. Even though Otto might have occasionally used strong-arm tactics to wrestle small grass-trampling children to the ground or to tackle elderly ladies who attempted to stuff flowers into their handbags, my article would not be completely true because it would leave the erroneous impression that Otto was a member of an amoral government organization that brutalized innocent people when he was actually a security guard at the tulip exhibit. Because of the false impression created by my characterization of his job, I would still be liable for defamation.

Chapter 2

Although a true statement cannot be the basis for a claim of defamation, a court can consider whether the circumstances under which that statement was made were inappropriate. It is possible to imagine situations in which one could say something that was completely true yet still be liable for some other tort such as the invasion of privacy or the intentional infliction of emotional distress. If I am a private citizen who likes to wear women's undergarments, the fact that you reveal this hobby at a party to celebrate my election to my church's board of trustees will not cause you to incur any liability for defamation if the statement about my fashion preferences is true. However, I might be able to sue you for invading my privacy because you revealed a private fact about me that served no useful purpose except to humiliate me. I might also be able to sue you for the intentional infliction of emotional distress if your remarks caused my spouse to become hysterical and thereby suffer great emotional trauma. Even if you made the statement because you thought it would help bolster my embryonic political career by showing transvestite voters that I was a man whom they could trust, your noble intentions would not insulate you from liability for either of the above-referenced torts.

Individuals may also be protected from liability if they enjoy an absolute privilege to say anything they want. Whether a statement by one who is absolutely privileged is motivated by spite or excessive hormone levels is irrelevant because the absence of a proper motive will not defeat an absolute privilege. Such privileges are granted to all of the participants in a trial, for example, including the judge, the attorneys, the witnesses, and the parties themselves because we want to facilitate the search for the truth. Many legal commentators believe that only by giving these participants the unfettered right to say anything they want can the ultimate issues of guilt or innocence be decided. Moreover, this absolute privilege will attach to all oral or written statements made in preparation for the trial such as depositions and interrogatories as well as those statements made following the rendition of a final verdict such as a motion to set aside the judgment. Although some courts have suggested that statements made during a judicial proceeding must bear some relationship to the cause of action, much discretion is afforded to the witness who wishes to ramble on about the character flaws of the defendant. It is more likely that an attorney or a judge will request that a witness limit his testimony to more relevant matters before the witness will be allowed to stray so far from the subject at hand that he might say something that would invalidate his privilege.

Legislators, by contrast, enjoy an absolute privilege that extends to all statements made during legislative sessions regardless of whether they bear any remote relationship to the subject being discussed. Consequently, a state legislator such as Joe-Bob Tilly could get up to speak about increased appropriations for education and declare that his secretary is a lesbian and that his former business partner stole money from a synagogue and that his brother eats cater-pillars without incurring any liability for defama-tion. The only significant restraint on Joe-Bob's ver-bal creativity will be the patience of the other legislators who might vote to gag their esteemed colleague.

A similar privilege exists for members of the ex-ecutive branch of government so long as the defam-atory statements are made while the speaker is ex-ercising the functions of her office. If the governor declares that a neighboring state's apples are in-fested with worms, her remarks will be absolutely privileged even though they bear no reasonable re-lationship to a pressing public issue and are not sup-ported by any proof. However, once the governor leaves office and becomes a spokeswoman for a private con-sortium of apple growers in her state, her dispar-aging remarks about the poor quality of the neigh-boring state's fruit will subject her to liability for defamation because she no longer enjoys an unqual-ified executive privilege.

People who like to talk with their spouses about the character flaws or the hideous appearances of their neighbors and friends will be pleased to know that their communications are absolutely privileged. However, this absolute privilege presupposes that the spouses are the only two persons present when the communications are made. If you are giving a speech about the need for better geriatric medical care to a large audience of elderly people and your spouse (who happens to be sitting next to you) asks that you pick up the pace so he does not have to continue listening to the "blue-haired blabbermouth" seated on his other side, the fact that his derogatory description of the woman is transmitted to the audience via your microphone will defeat the spousal privilege because it was communicated to third parties. Less clear is what sort of privilege would exist for a polygamist who has thirty-eight wives and declares that the family doctor is a doddering incompetent who could not diagnose a seasonal change. Because the focus of the privilege is on the marital relationship, it appears that such a communication would be absolutely privileged if only the polygamist and his bevy of wives were present when he made the statement. The presence of any other parties would serve to defeat the privilege.

Equal-time broadcasts will also be absolutely privileged when the broadcasting station or newspaper is legally required to permit all the candidates for a particular political office to speak to the voters. If there are three candidates for mayor on the ballot but one of them is a crackpot who favors passing a zoning ordinance that would require all residents to build a miniature replica of Stonehenge in their yards, then all three candidates must still be allowed to appear on the same broadcast. We do not want to give the manager of a broadcasting station the right to decide which candidate can appear because it would essentially permit her to censor the statements of the less conventional candidates. This absolute privilege may also extend to rebuttals given by third parties in response to editorials transmitted by a media defendant. One way to avoid any problems would be for the defendant to refuse to give broadcast time or newspaper space to any political candidates and to refrain from propagating its views about public issues so as to avoid the need to invite rebuttals. However, such an approach would not be favorably viewed by those long-winded do-gooders who believe that the media should provide information as well as entertainment to the public.

There are several situations in which one may make a defamatory statement without incurring liability owing to the existence of a qualified privilege. A qualified privilege will be available to those who report on public proceedings whether they relate to judicial trials, legislative sessions, or executive meetings. A reporter will be privileged to report a false statement that is made by one of the parties involved in such a proceeding but he will not be protected if he inaccurately reports the statement and thus defames an individual. If I am a television correspondent who is reporting on a special state legislative meeting called to debate whether to build a gigantic plastic bubble over our state to ensure that sunny weather prevails year-round, my report that a contractor bidding on the project said that those legislators against the project were being bribed by anti-plastic fanatics would be privileged. I would not be liable for reporting a defamatory statement accurately because it was made during a public proceeding. If I mistated the contractor's remarks, however, and attributed to him the claim that those legislators against the project were being bribed by the above-mentioned fanatics when the contractor merely stated that certain legislators were being heavily lobbied by special-interest groups, then my statement would not be privileged because my erroneous report contained a defamatory statement.

A qualified privilege will also exist for those who critique books, music, films, and other artistic works so long as the comments are relevant to the work being evaluated and do not become a springboard for making defamatory statements about the artist. As a reporter, I may comment on what I believe are the strengths and weaknesses of an exhibit of finger paintings by the noted artist Eric Rubbish at the Ostentatious Art Gallery, but I cannot go beyond my criticism of the art to suggest that the artist's use of murky colors shows that he beats his dog and is tormented by past crimes he committed involving moral turpitude. Such a personal barb is clearly beyond the scope of any legitimate criticism of the artist himself and is not really relevant to my analysis of the merits of the paintings themselves.

Statements made to public officials to facilitate their performance of their duties whether they involve issuing driver's licenses or registering voters will enjoy a limited privilege. If my explanation to a clerk at the driver's license office about an accident necessitates that I say several unflattering remarks about the driving ability of my next-door neighbor who actually caused the acident, then my statements will have a qualified privilege so long as they reasonably relate to my efforts to renew my driver's license. I will be free to point out that my next-door neighbor was steering his car with his knees and drinking a bottle of whiskey when he plowed into my car. I cannot then go on at length to speculate that my neighbor was probably the mastermind behind a recent string of liquor store robberies in the area simply because of the liquor bottle in his possession.

The statements I make on my own behalf to rebut a charge that I was rude to a customer while working at a local delicatessen, for example, will be privileged even if they contain defamatory statements about the customer's behavior in the store. However, I will lose that privilege if I begin to speculate that the customer's behavior was caused by certain chemical imbalances in his brain or his inability to attract members of the opposite sex because such speculations are not really relevant to my statements in defense of my own conduct. My explanation of my reaction to the behavior of the customer will be privileged, but I probably could not go on at great length speculating as to why the customer behaved in an offensive manner. The same reasoning would apply if I was trying to explain the conduct of a coworker who had been accused by a customer of being rude.

Invasion of Privacy

There are four causes of action that may be grouped together under the umbrella of *invasion of privacy torts,* and they include intrusion, commercial misappropriation of personality, disclosure of private facts, and false light privacy. The fundamental principles underlying these torts is that every person has an inherent right to privacy as well as the right to prevent the unauthorized use of her likeness for commercial purposes. In any event, these torts have developed over time to ensure that even the best-known personalities are able to enjoy some peace and quiet.

One commits the tort of intrusion by invading or otherwise intruding upon the plaintiff's solitude in a manner that is objectionable to an ordinary person. The invasion itself must be so intrusive that the defendant cannot argue that the plaintiff has somehow waived his right to privacy by his actions. If you are a beautiful model named Fabriqua Colonic, who models swimwear in the display window of a department store, my pressing my face against the window to leer at you for hours on end probably would not be regarded as intruding into your private affairs. You are modeling swimwear in a display window on a public street. It would be difficult for you to demonstrate that I had interfered with your solitude. However, you would be able to argue that I intruded upon your private affairs if you were bathing at home one evening and looked up to find me peering in the window at you. You would be within your rights to file an action against me for intrusion in such a situation because your bathing activities are within a sphere of privacy that has nothing to do with your modeling career. Consequently, you would probably succeed in your efforts to recover damages from me because I violated your reasonable expectation of privacy.

I could also commit the tort of intrusion by wiretapping your phones, intercepting your mail or digging through the contents of your locker at the department store. Whether I actually see or learn anything objectionable is of secondary importance because the tort of intrusion is primarily concerned with the mental anguish caused to the plaintiff by the objectionable conduct of the defendant.

The unauthorized appropriation of the plaintiff's likeness for commercial purposes will also give rise to liability for invasion of privacy. Despite its classification as a privacy tort, this cause of action is less concerned with privacy and more concerned with the right of an individual to control the commercial exploitation of her voice, likeness, etc. The damages that may be recovered might be limited to the amount of money generated by the unauthorized appropriation or they might be altered so as to compensate the plaintiff for the devaluation of his image caused by the unauthorized use of his likeness. If you are a famous athlete and I cut a picture of you out of a sports magazine and arrange it in an advertisement so that it appears you are enthusiastically recommending my company's new product, Spiffy Dog Chews, then I have used your photograph without permission as well as benefitted financially from my misbehavior. I was able to exploit the goodwill presumably engendered by your likeness to reach a wider audience without compensating you for its use. Whether I include a testimonial in the advertisement in which you brag that both you and your dog eat Spiffy Dog Chews is irrelevant as far as liability for the misappropriation is concerned. However, if the testimonial devalues your reputation or otherwise humiliates you, then it could affect the amount of damages awarded to you by a court.

Chapter 2

This is not to say that I will have misappropriated a famous person's likeness every time I publish her photograph in a newspaper or magazine because this tort usually arises in the context of commercial endorsements. A sports magazine covering a live grenade tossing tournament, for example, will not usually have to pay the featured (and surviving) athletes for the privilege of including their photographs in the magazine because the magazine is covering a sports event of interest to the public. It is not using these photographs to endorse particular products. The fact that the sports magazine makes a profit on that issue is irrelevant because the photographs were published to enhance the effectiveness of the magazine text.

One may also invade the privacy of another by publicly disclosing private facts about that person. To commit this tort, one must do more than merely intrude into a person's private affairs or disturb his solitude (intrusion); he must disclose to the public some sort of private information about the plaintiff that is so intimate that its publication would offend a person of ordinary sensibilities. The disclosure must be made to the general public via a newspaper or television or some other mass medium because a private disclosure such as a woman revealing to her mother the existence of her celebrity husband's heart-shaped tattoo will not be considered sufficient. Moreover, the facts disclosed must not already be of public record. If everybody already knew about the heart-shaped tattoo owing to the previous publication of an unauthorized biography about the celebrity husband, then there could be no disclosure because this particular fact was already known by the general public.

The unauthorized disclosure of private facts to the general public will not automatically create liability if the information is deemed to be sufficiently newsworthy. However, it is not always easy to decide what topics are of legitimate public interest. One of the most common situations involves the publication of private facts about a well-known personality whose life is already known to the public. Because this person is a household name, the story of her life is of interest to the public and she will probably be unable to prevent the disclosure of the same. However, she should be able to prevent the publication of particularly embarrassing or humiliating private facts that serve no legitimate public interest. The decision to prohibit the publication of the private facts will turn on whether the facts are so intimate that they would offend an ordinary person's sensibilities. Although this is admittedly something of a slippery standard, most people know what facts about themselves would cause them to suffer great embarrassment if these facts were to be disclosed to the public. Consequently, it is not difficult to apply a similar, albeit more relaxed, standard to celebrities. As with the tort of intrusion, the plaintiff does not need to prove that she has suffered pecuniary damages due to the disclosure but only that the disclosure has caused her mental anguish.

The defenses available to the defendant for disclosing private facts will include the consent of the plaintiff to the disclosure as well as any applicable absolute or qualified privileges discussed in the section on defamation. The fact that the facts are true is not a good defense because we are concerned not with a defamatory statement that injures the plaintiff's reputation but instead with the disclosure to the public of intimate details of the plaintiff's life that should remain private. If I report that you were once a member of a porcine cult, which dressed up in pink robes with curly tails and plastic snouts, such a revelation might prove to be embarrassing to you especially because this cult believes that the world will one day be conquered by hordes of pigs. If you are a private individual, you would probably be able to block the disclosure unless the revelation of your membership was incidental to an investigative report about porcine religious cults. If you were a celebrity whose exploits were constantly splashed across the tabloids, you might find it more difficult to obtain damages for such a disclosure because of the public's familiarity with your life. However, if a jury decided that no legitimate public interest was served by this disclosure, then you should be able to recover damages for the disclosure.

The fourth and final privacy tort may be committed by one who discloses true facts about the plaintiff in a manner that casts that person in a false light. The false impression must be offensive or otherwise objectionable to a reasonable person. However, no recovery will be permitted unless the facts creating the false light are actually disclosed to the public. In any event, the facts must be presented in such a manner to suggest falsely that the plaintiff has behaved in a particular manner or espoused certain views. If you are a well-known local politician who is wandering down a busy city street and you duck in a doorway to get out of the rain, the fact that I take your picture and my photograph shows you going into an unlicensed massage parlor could cast you in a false light if the photograph is published the next day accompanied by a caption suggesting that you are personally investigating the seven deadly sins. Because you intended merely to get out of the rain and had no desire to go sample the smorgasbord inside the parlor, my caption would cast you in a false light for which you could recover damages. The fact that I took a photograph of you walking into a massage parlor will not in itself constitute false light because I am within my rights to take photographs on public streets; it is the impression created by my caption that gives rise to my liability because it falsely suggests that you participate in illicit body rubs.

As with defamation, the public figure or public official will have to demonstrate that the actions creating the false light were made with knowledge of their falsity or with a reckless disregard for the truth. Private individuals, by contrast, will merely have to demonstrate that the reporter was negligent in her presentation of the facts that created the erroneous impression. As with the other privacy torts, the measure of damages will depend on the extent to which the plaintiff has suffered emotional distress. The plaintiff will not be required to show that he has suffered pecuniary damages from the disclosure.

CHAPTER 3

Negligence

---

*A little neglect may breed
mischief.*

— Benjamin Franklin

Chapter 3

3

No word will bring tears of joy to the eyes of a personal injury lawyer more quickly than the word *negligence*. Nothing will cause a corporate executive's blood to run cold quicker than the suggestion that her company's products have been negligently manufactured. Some people regard negligence as a legal device by which they can obtain huge sums of cash, whereas others view it as a primary reason for spiraling insurance rates. Although the attitudes toward the concept of negligence range from adulation to hostility, many people at either end of the spectrum have little knowledge about the basic elements of negligence.

To sustain a cause of action for negligence, the plaintiff must prove that (1) the defendant had a duty to act (2) in conformity with a particular standard of care (3) to protect the plaintiff against an unreasonable risk of harm (4) but the defendant breached that duty (5) and this breach was both a cause-in-fact and a proximate cause of the plaintiff's injury (6) that caused the plaintiff to suffer compensable damages. The plaintiff will also have to demonstrate that he did not behave in a negligent manner or otherwise assume the risk created by the defendant's negligent actions in order to prevail.

The Duty of Care

Any discussion of negligence must begin with the legal duty imposed by society on each individual to exercise the appropriate caution when engaged in activities that could result in harm to others. Of particular concern to legal scholars has been the extent to which a person owes a duty of care to the other members of society. Does this duty of care extend only to those persons one could foresee would be injured by the negligent performance of the dangerous activity or does this duty of care extend to all members of society? The answer to this question is important because it defines the parameters of liability that could be faced by a negligent defendant.

In general, a person owes a duty of care only to those people who could reasonably be expected to suffer injuries resulting from his breach of that duty. The problem with attempting to extend further the liability for breaching a duty of care is that there is no logical point at which liability may be cut off. Consequently, the courts have sought to limit liability to those persons who are in a foreseeable "zone of danger" when the defendant breaches his duty of care. If a baggage handler drops my package of fireworks while unloading it from a train and the package explodes, the baggage handler would be entitled to sue me for negligence because he was within the foreseeable zone of danger. It was reasonable to expect that a person handling a package filled with fireworks would be injured if the package exploded. Unless I could dissuade the baggage handler from suing me for negligence by challenging him to be a real man and stop whining about his third-degree burns, broken collar bone, and mangled arm, he should be able to establish that he was a foreseeable plaintiff who is entitled to recover for my negligence in shipping the fireworks on a passenger train.

The duty of care becomes somewhat more problematic if someone outside the immediate zone of danger tries to sue me for negligence. If the force of the explosion causes a pile of suitcases some distance away to topple onto my Aunt Agatha, then she might decide to cast aside any concerns with family loyalty and sue me for breaching my duty of care to her. However, Aunt Agatha's success in court will depend on whether she can show that it was reasonable to expect she would be injured by the explosion of the fireworks. If she proves that she was close enough to the explosion so that the force of the blast could knock the suitcase over, then she would probably prevail. The outcome would be less clear if there were several men with jackhammers digging up the concrete floor near the pile of suitcases when they fell over. This situation would cloud the causal relationship that might have otherwise been presumed to exist between the explosion and the suitcases falling onto my Aunt Agatha. This causal connection will become increasingly tenuous as the site of the accident becomes further removed from the explosion itself or the number of other potential causal agents increases. Aunt Agatha would have great difficulty arguing that my exploding package of fireworks caused her to suffer injury if the explosion occurred in Palm Beach and Aunt Agatha was pinned beneath a fine assortment of leather travel bags in Amsterdam. Similarly, if Aunt Agatha was standing in the same train station but she was separated from the exploding package by an oil-drilling rig, a coal mine, a sewer pipe being laid by the utility company, and a military bombing range, then her claim that my exploding package caused her injury would appear so farfetched that only one of Aunt Agatha's employees might seriously consider it. In any event, Aunt Agatha would have to demonstrate that she was in a foreseeable zone of danger in order to recover for her injuries.

The foreseeable plaintiff issue also arises when one person commits a negligent act that endangers another person thus prompting a rescue attempt by a third party. Because it is foreseeable that someone might try to rescue a person in distress, such good samaritans will be included in the class of foreseeable plaintiffs able to sue the negligent party for breaching her duty of care. If I play crack-the-whip with you while ice-skating for the first time on a frozen lake and one particularly vicious snap by you causes me to spin wildly out of control and fall through some ice marked with warning signs, then you would have arguably breached your duty of care to me. My calls for help might bring a kindhearted but somewhat pungent employee of a nearby chemical toilet factory onto the frozen lake. However, if my would-be rescuer falls through the ice while trying to extend his hand to me, then he would also be regarded as having been endangered by your negligence. Even though we both might find the numbing sensation of freezing water to be surprisingly therapeutic, you could be liable to both of us for negligence if we could demonstrate that the other elements of this cause of action exist.

What if there is no smelly third party around to rescue me? Then you will be faced with a moral dilemma of deciding whether to try to right your wrong and pull me out of the icy water or save your own skin and leave me to my own devices. Although you might feel some ethical obligation to rescue me, your even-stronger sense of self-preservation might cause you to bid me farwell and head back to the car before time expires on the parking meter so that you do not get a parking ticket. Because most people would find your behavior to be reprehensible, the law imposes a duty on you as the negligent party to make reasonable efforts to help protect me from suffering further injury. This affirmative duty might necessitate that you retrieve a tree branch and dash out onto the ice to rescue me. Even if I was partly responsible for my having ended up in the icy water, you would still be required to make some sort of reasonable effort to help me out of my predicament. The fact that you toss a seemingly buoyant steel girder to me will probably not be regarded as sufficient.

Liability may also be found for a failure to act when there is some sort of special relationship between the parties as would be the case with an innkeeper and her guests. If I am a guest at the River Styx Hotel and a light bulb in the lobby explodes causing the building to catch fire, the innkeeper cannot simply retrieve her fire insurance policy and leave the premises without making any attempt to get me as well as the other guests out of the building. Because I am a guest of the innkeeper, she must make a reasonable effort to help me get out of the building. This duty might be satisfied by knocking on all the doors and ringing the fire alarm. It would not be satisfied by the innkeeper mailing a letter to my home address informing me of the fire and the need to evacuate the hotel.

The above-described situations are exceptions to the general rule that liability for any resulting injuries will not be imposed on an individual who fails to rescue another person in peril. The fact that some curious onlookers gather onto the lake while I am still thrashing around in the icy water to place bets on how much longer I can continue to keep my head above the water will not exculpate you from liability for your negligent actions. More importantly, these voyueristic sporting enthusiasts are not required to toss a rope to me or make any other attempt to pull me out of the water. They could bring their folding chairs and picnic baskets out onto the ice and enjoy the spectacle and not worry about raising a finger because they have no duty to rescue me. The result would be different if I had originally been a member of the group and the negligent behavior of one of the other picnickers caused me to fall through the ice.

This protection from liability will not be extended to one who initiates an attempt to rescue another (despite the absence of any duty to do the same) but then changes his mind and terminates the rescue attempt thus leaving the victim in a worse situation. If one of the picnickers watching me thrash around in the water has a change of heart and decides to toss me a buoyant ice chest, the fact that the ice chest hits me on the head and knocks me out will not enable the picnicker to go back to his chair without a second thought because his rescue effort has left me in an even more perilous situation. I am now unconscious as well as drowning in a frozen lake. Moreover, the picnicker would also be liable for any injuries that he negligently caused while making his rescue attempt such as the concussion I suffered after being hit on the head.

The issue of liability for failure to act also arises when a person is the victim of a crime. It would appear that a town should be legally responsible for its failure to provide police protection to its citizens although nonresident visitors could be left to die on the streets. Does the victim of a robbery, for example, have any right to sue the town for failing to protect her from crime? Probably not. In general, a town enjoys immunity from suit for most causes of action unless there is a specific state statute to the contrary or the town has explicitly waived its immunity from suit. If I am robbed by an elderly lady who has just read the story of Robin Hood and desires to effect her own scheme of wealth redistribution, my suit against the town for failing to provide me with adequate police protection would probably be dismissed due to the inability of the town to guarantee the safety of every resident at all times. Because the town must decide how best to allocate its limited crime-fighting resources, it cannot be held responsible for all the crimes that do occur. Moreover, the courts would be reluctant to second-guess the decisions of the police department regarding the placement of available police officers because the courts would not know as much as the police about such matters. The same deference would be shown by the courts to the allocative decisions of any other municipal entity so long as the decisions appeared to have been reasonable when made.

Breaching the Duty of Care

To determine whether a duty of care has been breached, one has to ask whether the defendant's conduct was reasonable under the circumstances. This "reasonable person" standard appears throughout the law and provides the comparative scale for gauging the propriety of the defendant's actions. Although physical limitations will be taken into consideration when deciding whether a defendant exercised the appropriate degree of care, mental shortcomings will not be considered. We might ask whether a one-legged former sea captain, for example, who is now working as a waiter on roller skates in a drive-in theatre exercises the degree of care that we would expect from an ordinary one-legged drive-in theatre waiter. Our former sea captain would be expected to be aware of his physical limitations and govern his behavior accordingly. If he attempts to entertain the drive-in patrons during an intermission by dancing the can-can and one particularly vigorous kick sends his peg leg through both a windshield and the head of a patron, then our captain would be liable for his negligent action because he should have known that he could endanger a person by violently kicking his wooden leg into the air. By contrast, if the sea captain had a blot on his brain that caused him to begin shrieking at the top of his lungs every time he saw a motorcycle, his behavior would still be compared to that of a person of average intelligence. Consequently, mental impairments would not provide the sea captain with an excuse to avoid paying for the windshields that are cracked by his involuntary high-pitched screams.

The reasonable person standard also presupposes that the defendant has knowledge about those facts that are commonly known by ordinary persons in the community. If I believe that Aunt Agatha's butler, Charles, wears a magical suit to work every day that is impervious to fire, my belief, no matter how reasonable it appears to be to me, will not protect me from being sued for breaching my duty of care to Charles if I point and fire a flamethrower at his suit to test the validity of my theory. Because I am the only one who believes in magical suits, my erroneous assumption about the durability of his outfit will not be regarded as knowledge common to the other members of the community. Consequently, I will be seen as having departed from the standard of care that would be expected of an ordinary person of average intelligence in the locality. Nobody else believes in magical suits and only half of my fellow townspeople believe that rabbits lay colored eggs or that they can predict their futures based on the positions of the stars.

Not everybody is expected to conform to the reasonable person standard. A professional such as a doctor or a lawyer or a sidewalk hostess will be expected to possess the knowledge and exercise the degree of skill appropriate for a member of that profession. This standard of care will also be governed by the level of professional competence in the community. A surgeon in Timbuktu who, like the other doctors in her town, can only kill her patients by severing an artery with a machete, will not be compared with a Park Avenue surgeon who can kill his patients by making an almost invisible incision with a scalpel. Each surgeon's knowledge and skill will be compared against that possessed by her fellow surgeons in her community when deciding whether she exercised the appropriate degree of care. However, this locality rule will not necessarily be determinative as to whether a professional's conduct is appropriate but instead may be treated simply as a factor to be considered in deciding upon the proper standard of care. The reason for this is that the surgeons of Timbuktu may routinely commit malpractice and think nothing of it. We would not want to have the courts refusing to hold the surgeons in Timbuktu to a minimal level of competence owing to the fact that no Timbuktu surgeon has ever been competent.

Doctors who hold themselves out as specialists will be required to meet a national standard of compe-

tency and will not be able to defend their actions by
pointing to the low standards of their particular locality. If I am an expert in treating diseases of the
right leg and it is customary in my community for
physicians to treat leg problems ranging from vari-
cose veins to unwanted hair growth by amputation,
then I will not be able to defend my unblemished
record (of having treated every patient who has ever
set foot in my waiting room by hacking off his leg)
by reference to our rather unorthodox community
medical standards. Because I hold myself out as a
specialist in diseases of the right leg, my conduct will
be gauged by reference to the national standard of
competence for treating leg ailments.

The behavior exhibited by a child will usually be
compared to that possessed by other children of like
age, education, intelligence and experience to decide
whether the child has failed to exercise the appropriate degree of care. Most courts have adopted the
view that the child must be above a certain age before
he can be required to conform his behavior to a particular standard of conduct. However, many courts
have refrained from designating a specific age at which
the child is presumed to be responsible for his failure
to behave in an appropriate manner; the courts have
instead focused on what behavior should be expected
of a child of similar age, experience, education and
intelligence. If my ten-year-old nephew, Elvin, has
just learned how to play with matches and accidentally sets fire to a tree farm on my street, then Elvin's
failure to exercise the appropriate degree of care will
be assessed by trying to determine whether other ten-

year-olds could be expected to know the danger of lighting matches in the middle of a grove of trees. Although Elvin's age would probably save him from being sent to a labor camp to break large rocks into small rocks, a court would decide whether Elvin should be held liable for the damages caused by his actions by determining the appropriate behavior for a ten-year-old child like my nephew.

In the case of activities (such as driving a car) that are undertaken only by adults, however, Elvin would be held to the same standard of behavior as an adult driver. If Elvin decides to take one of Aunt Agatha's vintage motorcars out for a drive and he plows into the living room of a nearby house that somehow got in his way, he will not be able to claim that he should not be liable for the damages because very few ten-year-old children know how to drive an automobile. The court will decide whether Elvin's creation of a gaping hole for a picture window is the type of conduct that would be expected of the average adult driver. Assuming that Elvin's conduct falls short of that expected of the typical adult, he may be sent up to his room for the rest of his life.

If a person is unexpectedly confronted with an emergency, then due consideration will be given to the fact that he was not able to consider carefully his actions. However, this factor will not be taken into consideration if the emergency was created or otherwise exacerbated by that person's negligence. If I am pumping fuel into one of the massive tanks located beneath the gas station where I work and my lit cigarette is blown off a gas pump and into the tank thereby causing a massive explosion, my negligence in causing the accident would not excuse me for any subsequent acts of negligence I commit while trying to put out the fire. My inability to call the fire department on the phone, for example, might prompt me to climb into the station tow truck and, in my haste to get to the firehouse, knock a hole in the side of the garage thereby causing the roof to collapse. Because my careless placement of a lit cigarette was the cause of the explosion, my negligence in wrecking the garage will not be viewed any less severely even though I desperately wanted to drive over to the firehouse for help. If the explosion had been caused by the lit cigarette of my evil twin brother, however, then my ramming the side of the garage would be regarded with considerably less hostility by a court.

Doctors and nurses sometimes encounter medical emergencies not of their own making that require them to make snap judgments as to the appropriate form of treatment. A doctor who drives his car over to the side of a highway to assist an accident victim will often have very little time to consider the consequences of his actions. Because we want to encourage good samaritans to render medical assistance in such situations, many states have passed laws excusing medical professionals as well as other individuals from liability for ordinary negligence if the doctor has not treated the accident victim in the past and has no knowledge of her past medical history. In such a situation, a doctor will be liable only for gross negligence such as applying a tourniquet around the accident victim's neck to stop the bleeding of her left arm.

The duty of care issue also arises when trying to decide what duties a landowner owes to persons who venture onto his property. The key here is to focus not on the actual dangers that exist on the land or the injuries suffered by the visitor but instead on the legal status of the visitor. The fact that the land is abnormally dangerous is not so important in deciding whether a duty of care was breached; the status of the visitor as an invited guest or an unknown trespasser will be the most important factor in determining whether the landowner should be held responsible for any injuries suffered by the visitor.

A landowner will generally not be held responsible for natural conditions on his property that somehow infringe on the possessory interests of neighboring property owners or other persons who happen to be on the affected lands. If there is a nest of very large dragonflies on my property and they periodically "buzz" the rooftops of the neighbors, then my neighbors will probably be unable to assert that I am required under the law to protect them against these low-flying nuisances because the dragonflies are a natural condition of the land. The outcome would be different, however, if I bought some steroid-treated dragonflies that were as large as surfboards and one of them carried off my neighbor's children. In such a situation, I would not be able to argue that the presence of the dragonflies was a natural condition of the land because I was responsible for the placement on my property.

In general, I do not have a duty to protect persons outside my property from artificial conditions on my land. However, I could be held liable for damages caused by unreasonably dangerous artificial conditions on my property that lie in close proximity to adjacent lands. My property might have a rotting woodshed with nail-laden planks that could pose a danger to small children playing in the next yard. Even if the woodshed was erected on the property before I purchased the land, I would still be responsible for protecting my neighbors from the dangers posed by the woodshed. Consequently, I would be required to take whatever steps were necessary to ensure that persons on the adjacent lands would not be injured by the planks. I would be afforded great discretion in how I chose to resolve the problem so long as I did not unreasonably endanger the safety of others. I could hire a meticulously dressed group of exterior decorators to dismantle the woodshed by carefully prying each plank off the frame and removing each nail or I could hire a sloppily attired group of demolition experts to blow up the decrepit structure. However, the latter approach would send a shower of wooden splinters in all directions that could injure persons working in their gardens or reclining by their pools. As a result, I might have to choose a less flamboyant way of dismantling the woodshed.

As a landowner, I must also refrain from engaging in excessively dangerous activities on my land that could harm people outside my property. If I live at Barrymore Estate, an aging neo-Gothic mansion in an affluent community peppered by other large, creaky residences, I cannot do anything I want on my property without considering the impact my activities might have on the adjacent properties. Similarly, I cannot permit my visitors to engage in any activities they choose if their conduct might pose a danger to persons outside my property. If I finally realize my lifelong dream of building a poisonous snake pit next to my house, I must exercise the appropriate degree of care to ensure that these beasts do not escape and visit my neighbors. As a result, I cannot allow my snakes to get their exercise each day by opening the pen and allowing them to slither wherever they want because they could easily disappear into the woods and reappear in someone else's yard. Moreover, I must control the conduct of the other members of the local reptile club when they visit me with their poisonous snakes, and I must do whatever is necessary to prevent them from letting their rattlesnakes and cobras slither around the yard so as to avoid endangering my neighbors.

The duty of care owed by myself to any person venturing onto my property will depend on whether that person is a trespasser, a licensee, or an invitee. My liability for any injuries caused to my visitor will depend more on whether my visitor was invited or anticipated than the nature of the actual injuries suffered by him. Because trespassers enjoy the fewest rights in the hierarchy of privileges afforded to those who venture onto real property owned by another, they represent an appropriate place to begin our discussion of what responsibility will be imposed on the landowner for injuries occurring to other people on his land.

Chapter 3

A trespasser is any person who goes onto the land of another without permission. Because almost everyone has trespassed at one time or another in his or her criminal career, it is difficult to generalize as to the genetic factors that may predispose one toward infringing upon the property rights of others. Moreover, one cannot point to any particular set of physical features such as beady eyes or thinning hair as being commonly found on those who trespass. Fortunately, one does not need to worry about undiscovered trespassers because they are owed no duty of care by the landowner. Even though you might sneak onto my property every so often to photograph my dragonflies, I am not obligated to wander around my property to warn you of any unreasonably dangerous conditions on my land because I have no knowledge of your presence. Once I discover your presence on my property, however, I am obligated to make reasonable efforts to inform you of any unreasonably dangerous artificial conditions that exist on the property. If a large pit on my land is concealed by dense undergrowth, I would be obligated to post signs around the pit warning of the danger or perhaps put up a fence around it. If you were extremely stubborn or perhaps made it a daily practice to ignore warning signs and fell into the pit, you would have no cause of action against me because I cannot be responsible for your bizarre behavior once I have taken reasonable steps to protect any discovered trespassers venturing onto my property. Your position would be even weaker if the pit had been created by a glacier that cut through my property because I have no duty to protect you from the natural hazards of the land. Furthermore, I would not have a duty to protect you from artificial conditions on the land that did not pose a significant risk of bodily harm such as a sandbox filled with crickets. The fact that you trip over the sandbox and are suddenly covered with crickets might cause you to suffer great emotional distress but that is not the type of harm that would necessitate any affirmative duties be imposed on me to protect you.

Anticipated trespassers are generally owed the same duty of care as discovered trespassers. An anticipated trespasser is one who the landowner suspects ventures onto his land from time to time. If I have a chocolate well on my property and it is the only source of that precious food for miles around, then the fact that I see other people walking down the street in front of my house carrying buckets of freshly drawn chocolate would give me good reason to suspect that it was being obtained from my well. The fact that I did not actually observe these people lowering their buckets down into the chocolate well would not allay my suspicions because determining whether one is an anticipated trespasser often depends on circumstantial evidence.

The last category of trespassers are small children who are too young to appreciate the dangers of artificial conditions on lands owned by another. This artificial condition does not need to be inherently dangerous but it must be something that could pose a significant risk of harm to small children who are too young to appreciate its potential hazards. The attractive nuisance doctrine imposes a duty on the landowner to take reasonable measures to protect young children venturing onto his property from being injured by the artificial condition. If I keep a massive abandoned tire collection in my yard to raise the dander of my snobby neighbors, I am required by law to take reasonable measures to prevent young children venturing onto my property from suffering any foreseeable injuries. A child who is injured while playing on my tires must demonstrate that there was a known dangerous artificial condition on my land and that I knew small children sometimes ventured onto my land to recover damages from me. She must also show that she was unable to appreciate the risk posed by the artificial condition and that the cost of protecting her from harm was minor compared with the injury she suffered. The focus is on the inability of the child to appreciate the risk of injury posed by the artificial condition. If several of my poisonous snake collector friends snuck onto my property after having a few too many drinks and started climbing up the pile of tires but one of them fell off the top and injured himself, then he could not argue that I had a duty of care to protect him. It was his drunken condition—not his physical age—that prevented him from appreciating the danger posed by the tire pile.

The attractive nuisance doctrine was developed to protect children who are too young to understand potential hazards. It does not apply to adults who voluntarily render themselves incapable of understanding these hazards by consuming large quantities of alcoholic beverages. Children do not have to be attracted onto the land in order to activate the duty of care of the landowner; the fact that one could reasonably anticipate that an artificial condition such as a swimming pool could harm a young child provides the basis for holding the landowner responsible for any resulting injuries.

As the landowner, I might be able to escape liability if the tires had been left on my property by a third party. If my gardener, Otto Hertz, had stored some old tires on my land without first obtaining my permission, then a trespassing child suffering injury from the tires would have the right to proceed against Otto directly because Otto was responsible for the tires being placed on my property. Any liability that I might incur owing to my having given Otto permission to store the tires on my property would be secondary if it existed at all.

Licensees rank somewhat higher than trespassers in the eyes of wealthy property owners because a licensee must obtain the permission of the landowner before venturing onto his property in order to be treated as such. A licensee may be defined as one whose venture on the land of another is motivated by a desire to obtain some sort of pecuniary benefit for herself rather than to confer a benefit on the landowner. If you are at a black-tie cocktail party attended by many overdressed wealthy people, it is considered much more advantageous to declare that you are a licensee instead of a trespasser even if you must fudge the truth because wealthy people hate trespassers almost as much as they hate lawyers. Trespassers are seen as having no regard for the property rights of others, whereas licensees are viewed in a somewhat more favorable light because they at least take some steps to get permission before going onto the land of another.

Because a licensee is someone who ventures the land of another to benefit himself primarily, a door-to-door salesman hauling a set of encyclopedias around on his back would be considered a licensee. His ringing my doorbell is prompted mainly by his desire to make a commission from selling me a set of books. However, the benefit realized by the licensee does not have to be pecuniary in nature. If I throw a conformity theme party in which all the guests come dressed in business suits, each guest is considered to be a licensee even though I may derive some personal satisfaction from the attendance of so many of my casual acquaintances (who could care less whether I live or die so long as I have adequately stocked the bar). I am required by law to warn my guests of any dangerous conditions on my land that could pose an unreasonable risk of harm to them when it is unlikely that my guests would actually be aware of the dangerous conditions. If all of my guests are familiar with the poisonous snake pit, the pile of tires, the woodshed, and the pit on my property, then I may not be required to make any additional warnings because they already know about these hazards and presumably will have the sense to avoid them. However, I am not required to inspect these hazards periodically for needed repairs or actually make repairs to satisfy my duty of care to my guests.

Unlike a licensee, an invitee is one who is invited by the landowner onto his property to benefit the landowner in some tangible way. In the case of a private landowner, an invitee might be an employee of the landowner or perhaps someone delivering an item to the landowner such as a package or an appliance. Santa Claus would probably be considered an invitee if he slid down the chimney of my home to leave some presents under the tree because his primary purpose in landing his sleigh on my roof is to confer a benefit on me in the form of the presents. Yet if Santa Claus had fallen on hard times in recent years and was now stealing valuables from those very same homes, he could no longer be considered an invitee because his visits would no longer primarily benefit the owners. In fact, his attempts to steal valuables from homes would cause him to be treated as a trespasser and a burglar because nobody gave him permission to enter their home to "make a profit" on Christmas Eve. I would then have no choice but to have Santa Claus arrested and his reindeer sold to a local petting zoo.

An invitee may also be one who visits the property of another that is open to the general public. If I buy a ticket to go visit the Museum of Sanitation, which boasts a number of displays showing the evolution of modern garbage-collecting technologies, I would be considered an invitee because I was on the property for the particular purpose for which it was open to the public. If I was a door-to-door salesman selling trash bags, however, and I entered the property to try to sell a box of bags to the museum curator, I would be regarded as a mere licensee because I was on the land not to confer a benefit on the museum in the form of my paid attendance but instead to sell my products and thus earn a commission. If I was ordered to leave the premises owing to my rather overbearing sales pitch but I then snuck back into the museum to make one final plea to the curator, I would no longer be treated as even a licensee but instead as a trespasser owing to my unwanted intrusion onto the premises.

A landowner must notify the invitee of any dangerous conditions on the land of which he is aware as well as take reasonable measures to conduct potentially dangerous activities on his land in a prudent manner. Unlike a licensee, however, a landowner owes an invitee the additional duty to make reasonable inspections to discover and remedy dangerous conditions on the land. If a delivery driver shows up at my front door to drop off my new piano, he would be regarded as an invitee because his delivery is of primary benefit to myself. Consequently, I am obliged to make periodic inspections of my property to protect the delivery driver and other invitees from any hazards that might pose considerable risks to their physical well-being. These hazards must be considered as such by reasonable persons. If my yard contains several songbird nests and the delivery driver believes that songbirds are vile, people-eating creatures that can spit a stream of flame the length of a football field, I would not be responsible for chasing off the songbirds before the delivery driver set foot on my property with my piano. His belief is clearly not reasonable because very few songbirds have ever eaten a human being and even fewer songbirds in this select group would be inclined to sample the dingy flavor of a cigar-smoking delivery driver. Because the songbirds do not pose a danger to the life of the delivery driver, I would not have to wander around the grounds of my property with a net and pointed stick to frighten off any songbirds before the delivery driver was obliged to hand over my piano.

A different outcome would result if the delivery driver had to drive his truck over a creaky wooden bridge at the base of my driveway to get to my home. I would be required to have the bridge inspected by an engineer every so often to verify that it was structurally sound. If I decided to dispense with the inspections because the bridge hardly sways when children ride their bicycles over it, then I would be liable for any injuries suffered by the delivery driver if the bridge collapsed when he drove his truck over it. Although I might try to cloud the issue of liability by running outside and accusing the dazed delivery driver of having destroyed my antique bridge, I would not be able to avoid responsibility for my failure to inspect the bridge for defects. If I wished to avoid inspecting the bridge for the foreseeable future because I had just finished building a new bridge (thus rendering the old bridge useless to me), I could try to protect myself by posting a warning sign on the old bridge and perhaps erecting a small gate on the street side of the bridge to prevent anyone from using it. The fact that the delivery driver could not read the warning sign or deliberately crashed through the gate to test the durability of his truck bumper would prevent him from claiming that I had somehow failed to make the necessary inspections of the potentially hazardous condition. The courts will not hold the landowner legally responsible when the licensee or invitee is determined to test the limits of his own mortality.

Although the landowner is the party charged with the duty to protect visitors from injury, this responsibility may devolve to any party leasing the property from the landowner because the lessee will necessarily assume day-to-day control of the property. The question as to who shall bear liability for an injury occurring on the land may be answered by determining who has the right to possess the land. A landowner who leases his land does not have the right to possess his property so long as the lessee complies with the terms of the lease. If I lease some of my land to Dominique Thunderbolt (who has just taken a correspondence course in dredging) so that she may practice her newly acquired skills by digging holes with a steam shovel and then filling them up again, I will have relinquished my day-to-day control over that portion of my property. The fact that Miss Tuttleworth falls into one of Dominique's partly-filled holes while she is en route to my house to complain about my having painted the front gate a bright orange color, should cause Dominique to be held responsible for any injuries suffered by Miss Tuttleworth so long as the injury actually occurred on the leased land. By signing the lease, Dominique agreed to maintain the leased property in a manner that would not endanger the lives of others. If Miss Tuttleworth came to visit Dominique to buy a bag of potting soil (and thereby confer a pecuniary benefit on Dominique—thus making Miss Tuttleworth an invitee of Dominique), Dominique would also be required to make periodic inspections of the digging area on the leased land and correct any dangerous artificial conditions to protect her visitors from harm. However, I would still be liable for any injuries suffered by Miss Tuttleworth on the lands that I did not lease to Dominique because I would be the one who had day-to-day control over those lands.

My ability to shift the liability for the dangerous conditions on the leased land to Dominique or any other lessee may depend on my having disclosed to the lessee the existence of any dangerous conditions that the lessee is unlikely to discover on her own. If the leased property included a small hut with a dirt floor that concealed a spring trap, I would be obliged to inform Dominique of the existence of the trap because she might not see it before tripping it and suffering great injury. Moreover, if I had agreed as part of the lease to make repairs on the hut and had reserved the right to enter the hut whenever it was convenient to me to make the repairs, then I would still be liable for any injuries caused by my failure to make those repairs. Had I failed to agree to make repairs on the hut as part of the lease agreement, I would still be liable if I entered the hut of my own free will to make the repairs gratuitously but failed to correct the defect.

Although many of us are concerned about what we must do to protect ourselves from being sued by clumsy oafs who trip over logs or fall out of trees on our property, many more of us need to know what we must do to avoid being sued by people who ride with us in our automobiles. Under the common law, the "guests" (nonpaying riders) of automobile owners were owed the same duty of care as a landowner owed to a licensee in that the automobile owner was required to warn the guest of any known defects in the vehicle and operate it in a reasonable manner. Many states have enacted so-called guest statutes that impose liability on the driver for injuries caused to the guest rider only if the driver's operation of the vehicle is reckless. Those persons who actually pay the driver for the privilege of riding in his car are considered to be "passengers" instead of guests; the driver is obliged to exercise ordinary care to protect passengers and will be liable for any injuries resulting from his failure to do so. If Aunt Agatha asks me to drive her to the beauty parlor for her monthly facial reconstruction because she recently sacked her chauffeur, my agreement to take her to Jean Pierre, the master of facial plaster, will cause Aunt Agatha to be considered a guest of mine in my automobile because I will not be charging her for the trip. Consequently, I would be liable to Aunt Agatha only for any injuries she suffers that are caused by reckless behavior on my part such as my driving with my eyes closed. If I accidently ran the car over a rock in the road thereby causing Aunt Agatha to bump her head, however, I would not be liable for her head injury because it resulted from what was, at most, negligent driving on my part. My hitting a small rock in the road would not be regarded as reckless conduct because I did not act with the requisite degree of carelessness. In any event, Aunt Agatha would have to ply me with many unbrella-laden tropical drinks before I would be disoriented enough to drive in a manner sufficiently reckless to incur liability for her injuries. The situation would be somewhat different if Aunt Agatha decided to pay me a small fee for my trouble because she would then be considered a passenger under the law and I would be obliged to exercise a reasonable duty of care in the operation of my automobile to avoid liability for any injuries to my Aunt Agatha.

Many states have adopted statutes providing for the imposition of a criminal penalty if the violator fails to conform his behavior to a certain standard of care. Because these laws are more precise in spelling out the particular standard of care that must be exercised as well as the party entitled to maintain a cause of action, it is often advantageous for a plaintiff to pursue a claim for a breach of a statutory duty of care. To succeed in such a claim, the plaintiff must demonstrate that she is a member of the class that the statute was designed to protect and that she has suffered the harm that the statute was designed to prevent. In addition, the plaintiff must also demonstrate that the statute was drafted in a manner so that anyone reading it would know what types of conduct it was designed to prevent as well as the penalties for such conduct. In short, the statute must be clearly worded and unambiguous. A violation of such a statute will constitute *negligence per se,* which means that the plaintiff will have shifted to the defendant the conclusive presumption that a duty of care existed and that the defendant breached that duty. The defendant may escape liability by showing that his conduct was excused because his own particular circumstances made it impossible for him to comply with the statute or that his behavior—though constituting a technical violation of the statute—was undertaken to avoid the greater injury that would have resulted from strict compliance with the statute. If I go out for a walk on a busy city street with my pet armadillo and I am waiting at a crosswalk for the light to change, the fact that a gigantic gorilla falls off the building right behind me would justify my rushing out into the street to get out of its way. Even though there might be a statute explicitly prohibiting jaywalking, my conduct would be excused because it is certainly preferable that I dash around several cars instead of soften the landing of a fifty-ton gorilla. Jaywalking enables me to avoid the greater harm that would result from my steadfastly maintaining my position at the streetcorner as the gorilla plummeted toward me. The fact that there is a very remote chance that the gorilla might suddenly sprout wings so that he could fly away and thus avoid flattening me and my armadillo will not be considered because we are concerned with real-world probabilities and not the speculations of a few half-witted zoologists.

Having immersed ourselves in the duty of care, the next step in deciding whether a negligence action can be maintained is to determine whether there was an actual breach of that duty. The plaintiff may demonstrate that the defendant acted in an unreasonable manner and that his conduct was not excused. The court may have to refer to the customs in a particular trade or industry or even a statutory standard to decide whether the defendant acted in an unreasonable manner. If there is a statute governing the way in which one should handle a blowtorch when repairing an elevator, for example, then my climbing aboard a crowded elevator with my flaming blowtorch in one hand and my blasting powder in the other hand would probably run afoul of the safeguards outlined in the statute. In the absence of an applicable statute, the court could look to the operating techniques of other blowtorch operators to determine the appropriateness of my actions.

A breach may also be found based on circumstantial evidence. The doctrine of *res ipsa loquitur* permits a plaintiff to demonstrate that the defendant has breached his duty of care when the situation is such that the injury could not have resulted unless the defendant was negligent. For *res ipsa loquitur* to apply, the plaintiff must show that the outcome could not have occurred in the absence of negligence and that the instrumentality that caused the result was controlled by the defendant. The plaintiff must also demonstrate that she did not act in a manner that contributed to the outcome. *Res ipsa loquitur* permits a court to infer that a breach of duty of care has occurred when the situation is such that no other logical conclusion can be drawn. A plane crash is an event to which *res ipsa loquitur* can be applied because the fact that the crash occurred creates the

Chapter 3

presumption that someone such as the pilot was negligent. Moreover, the plane itself was controlled solely by the flight crew. Short of the defendant being able to demonstrate that the plaintiff somehow contributed to the accident, the plaintiff should be able to establish a prima facie case of negligence in such a situation.

Res ipsa loquitur would also be applicable if Otto and I were out in my yard practicing the ancient art of shovel-tossing and one particularly errant toss of the spade by myself ended with the shovel burying itself in the ribs of the postman who had just arrived with the morning mail. The postman could show that I breached my duty of care by establishing that one does not usually find a shovel planted in the ribs of another person unless someone was negligent. The postman would then have to show by circumstantial evidence that I was in exclusive control of the shovel when I tossed it in the postman's direction and that he did not actually run out of his way to get hit by the shovel. Because Otto would be happy for the right price to accuse me of having tossed the shovel as well as committed a dozen assorted murders, the postman probably would not have too much difficulty establishing that I was negligent.

Causation

After the plaintiff demonstrates that the defendant has breached a duty of care, he must then demonstrate that there is a causal connection between the breach and the injury suffered by the plaintiff. Before determining whether the defendant's conduct is a proximate cause of the plaintiff's injury, however, the plaintiff must show that the defendant's conduct actually caused his injury. The "but for" test may be used by the plaintiff to show that his injury could not have occurred in the absence of the defendant's conduct. As a result, the postman could argue that but for my having flung the shovel in his direction, he would not have been speared. Such a situation would provide a clear-cut example in which a single causal agent resulted in a single outcome. However, the "but for" test would not be so helpful if my shovel hit the postman at the same time that thirty other shovels thrown by other shovel-tossers practicing with me struck him. Assuming that no one could tell whose shovel had caused what injury to the postman, the "but for" test would be of little help in resolving the issue of who was liable for negligence.

In cases where more than one causal factor simultaneously brings about a single outcome, the "substantial factor" test may be used to determine whether one should be liable for negligence. If the postman can show that my shovel was a substantial factor in causing his injury, then he does not need to demonstrate that he would not have suffered such an injury had I not flung my shovel at him. The fact that my shovel was only one among many stuck in his body will not obligate the postman to show which injuries to his person were caused by my shovel due to the impossibility of separating the damages caused by my shovel from the damages caused by all the other shovels that struck the postman. Once the postman is able to prove that his injuries resulted from being struck by the shovels, the burden of proof will then shift to me and the other defendants to prove that we were not at fault. Although each shovel-tosser is liable only for those damages that were caused by his particular shovel, the impossibility of separating the actions of the defendants from the postman's injuries necessitates that the liability for his injuries be parceled out among the defendants in some manner. It is less burdensome to require each of the wrongdoers to bear the burden of proving that they were not responsible for the injuries; the plaintiff should not be forced to prove his case against each of the defendants when their negligent actions cannot be separated from the plaintiff's injuries. If thirty shovel-tossers including myself hit the postman with our shovels, then the court might avoid the causation issue altogether by deciding that each of us should pay for one-thirtieth of the damages suffered by the postman.

Once the issue of factual causation has been addressed, the negligence analysis must move on to the question of proximate or legal causation. The requirement that the defendant's negligence be a proximate cause of the injury suffered by the plaintiff represents a limitation on the defendant's liability for certain unanticipated consequences of his actions. More specifically, we might ask if there is some intervening event that acts to sever the causal chain between the defendant's negligence and the plaintiff's injury or if the injury is so remote or unforeseeable that it is unconscionable to hold the defendant responsible.

Chapter 3

Proximate causation may be better understood by considering the concept of direct causation in which there is no break in the causal chain between the defendant's negligence and the plaintiff's injury. If there is no intervention by any third party that would prevent an observer from tracing the injury directly back to the negligent action, then the negligence of the defendant is a direct cause of the plaintiff's injuries, and the defendant will be liable for those injuries regardless of whether they were foreseeable. If my burying the pointed end of my shovel in the ribs of the postman causes him to drop to the ground thereby jamming the handle of the shovel into a gas line buried just a few inches beneath the grass, I would be responsible for the resulting gas explosions that level several homes in my neighborhood. Even though I could have never anticipated that a half dozen mansions would be blown up by my negligently tossing my shovel in the postman's direction, I would be held liable for those consequences owing to the uninterrupted causal chain. The fact that I could not have foreseen the nature or extent of the damages or the manner by which they were caused will not somehow dilute my liability for the damages. The gas explosions would not have occurred had I not plunged my shovel into the postman so a court would be within its power to hold me responsible for the damages to all of the homes of my former neighbors.

The issue of causation becomes somewhat more cloudy when intervening events come into play between the time that the defendant committed the negligent action and the time that the plaintiff suffered his injury. These intervening causes may or may not insulate the defendant from his negligent actions depending on whether these causes are foreseeable. The issue of foreseeability will be resolved by determining whether it was reasonable to anticipate that the intervening cause might manifest given the particular circumstances surrounding the defendant's actions. If the intervening cause is indeed foreseeable, then the defendant will remain liable for the injuries caused to the plaintiff because the causal chain has not been broken. If you run over my gardener, Otto Hertz, and break his leg while driving up to my house to visit me, you would be liable for any aggravation of Otto's injuries caused by the incompetent medical treatment rendered by his dockworker-turned-physician, Dr. Frank. The fact that Otto had freely chosen Dr. Frank to be his physician and rejected your offer to set his leg personally is not relevant. Your actions caused Otto to suffer a broken leg; it was foreseeable that he would seek medical treatment for his injuries and that his doctor might be incompetent. Had his leg not been broken, there would have been no need for him to subject himself to the unorthodox techniques practiced by Dr. Frank. Similarly, if your car had simply dragged Otto along the driveway for several hundred feet until he rolled onto the road and fell into a deep ravine, then my attempt to rescue Otto by dropping an aluminum ladder into the ravine (which strikes him on the head and knocks him unconscious) will not excuse you from liability for your original actions. Your negligence caused Otto to end up in the ravine, and it was foreseeable that some noble soul such as myself would try to rescue Otto by tossing a ladder or a rope to him. The fact that my rescue attempt may have been somewhat flawed will not excuse you from your original negligent actions.

An unforeseeable intervening cause, on the other hand, will supersede the defendant's actions so that she will not be deemed to have proximately caused the plaintiff's injuries. This superseding event will break the causal connection between the defendant's actions and the plaintiff's injuries and will thus be considered the direct cause of those injuries. As a result, the defendant may no longer be liable to the plaintiff. Some of the more common examples of superseding causes include torts and crimes committed by third parties as well as acts of God. The existence of a superseding event will excuse the defendant from liability for the plaintiff's injuries when the event cannot be regarded as foreseeable. If Otto and I go out for a drive in an automobile with bad brakes, we might turn onto a sloping road on which the maniacal tree surgeon Oscar O'Grady is cutting down some rare Antarctic pine trees. If the brakes give out thus causing us to roll down the road at an ever-increasing speed, the fact that we do not come to a halt until one of the pine trees crashes down onto the car and injures Otto may excuse my negligence in failing to have the brakes repaired because it was not foreseeable that we would get struck by a tree that was illegally cut down by a crazed tree surgeon. Oscar O'Grady's actions would probably be regarded as a superseding cause that would snap the causal chain between my failure to repair the brakes and the injuries suffered by Otto.

If a superseding cause manifests but the actual outcome is one that could have been expected to result from the defendant's negligence, then the defendant will probably still be liable for his actions. If Otto and I go out for a drive in the automobile with the bad brakes and we are swept up in the swirling winds of a tornado and carried through the air for a long distance until being dropped onto another sloping road, the fact that the brakes then give out completely and Otto and I crash into an embankment at the bottom of the hill and suffer substantial injuries will not necessarily excuse me from my failure to have the brakes repaired. The fact that it was unforeseeable that a tornado would carry us through the air would not be relevant because the tornado did not cause the brakes to malfunction; the brakes did not work even before we started our drive. Consequently, I could be liable to Otto for any injuries he suffered from the crash into the embankment because that result was foreseeable due to my failure to repair my brakes.

Damages

The plaintiff seeking to maintain an action for negligence must also show that she has suffered damages from the defendant's negligence. These damages may include the costs of the plaintiff's medical expenses as well as any lost earnings and compensation for her pain and suffering. Because the amount of damages for personal injuries will necessarily include past as well as future costs that may be attributed to the defendant's negligent actions, the calculation of a precise amount is not always possible. However, the court hearing the claim will try to decide what amount of money will fully compensate the plaintiff for her injuries. The court will also include in that total any damage to the plaintiff's property caused by the defendant's negligence. However, the plaintiff cannot recover damages for purely economic injuries because she has not suffered personal injury or sustained damage to her property. An employee of a newsstand demolished by your blindfolded drive through a parking lot would not be able to recover his lost wages from you even though he would be out of work for several weeks while the newsstand is being rebuilt because his injury is purely economic. He did not suffer any personal injury nor did he own the business that you destroyed. However, you would be liable to the owner of the newsstand because she did suffer property damage due to your negligence. If your plowing into the newsstand also caused the owner to suffer severe emotional distress because she erroneously believed that one of her employees was inside, then you might also be liable for any resulting psychological damages suffered by the owner so long as she exhibited some physical symptoms of the emotional trauma.

Defenses

There are several defenses that may be offered by a negligent defendant that, if proven, may defeat the plaintiff's cause of action. If the plaintiff acts in an unreasonable manner that causes him to suffer harm, his claim of negligence against the defendant may be barred. As with the negligent defendant, the actions of the plaintiff will be examined using an objective standard to determine whether his conduct fell below an acceptable standard. However, the plaintiff's contributory negligence must be both an actual cause as well as a proximate cause of the plaintiff's injury or else it will not provide the defendant with a defense to the plaintiff's original cause of action. If I began chopping down some tall trees because I wanted to see what it was like to be a lumberjack, the fact that I did not pay any attention to how I was angling my chops would result in my being liable for negligence if one of the trees crushed Otto's garden house and injured him. I would clearly be liable for any property damages sustained by Otto as well as his personal injuries. However, if Otto ran into the garden house solely to film the massive trunk crashing through his ceiling, then Otto would be contributorily negligent because he would not have sustained personal injury had he not tried to capture the moment on film. The result would be different, however, if Otto went into his house to save his three-year-old nephew from the falling tree because Otto's conduct was both reasonable and foreseeable under the circumstances. If that were the case, I would still be liable for Otto's personal injuries as well as any property damage.

Because the contributory negligence of the plaintiff will bar her right to recover damages from the defendant, many states have developed alternative approaches to avoid this harsh result including the last clear chance doctrine and the concept of comparative negligence. The last clear chance doctrine permits a plaintiff who is contributorily negligent to recover from a negligent defendant if the defendant had the final opportunity to prevent the injury suffered by the plaintiff. If I walk onto a railroad track to look for uprooted ties to augment my collection of rust-covered knicknacks, my scampering along the rails might be considered contributorily negligent because I had consciously put myself into a potentially dangerous situation. The situation might be further complicated if I could not hear the warning whistles of an oncoming trail because I was listening to loud music on a radio headset. If the engineer saw me in time to stop the train but failed to do so, his failure to act would render the railroad liable for negligence only if the engineer knew that I was not aware of the oncoming train. Because I could have easily stepped off the track had I bothered to pay attention, I would have to show that the engineer had actual knowledge of my inattentiveness before I could recover damages from the railroad.

A different standard would apply if I had caught my foot in the rail so that I was unable to get off the railroad track without assistance. My contributory negligence would not bar me from suing the railroad for shoving me along on a cowcatcher for ten miles if I could show that the engineer either knew that I was helpless or should have known that I could not free myself. If I could meet either test, then the court hearing my claim would probably rule that the engineer had the last clear chance to avoid the accident but failed to do so. Such a finding would enable me to proceed against the railroad due to the engineer's negligent operation of the train.

If the situation had been different, however, and the train was being driven by a psychotic engineer who wore patches over both eyes because he believed he was twice as fierce as any other make-believe pirate, then my failure to get off the track as I watched the train rumble into view (assuming that I was able to do so) would mean that I had the last clear chance to avoid the accident. Because I failed to take advantage of the opportunity to get out of the path of the train, I would not be able to recover for the injuries caused to my person by the train because I was contributorily negligent.

Imputed contributory negligence usually arises in situations where an employee's negligence causes him to become involved in an accident with another party who is also negligent. If the employee's boss attempts to sue the other party for negligence, then the other party may raise the employee's contributory negligence as a defense and it will be imputed to the employer thereby barring his suit. In such a situation, the court will transfer the contributory negligence of the employee to the employer if the employee was acting within the scope of his employment at the time of the accident. Contributory negligence will be imputed only when the party bringing suit and the one to whom the contributory negligence would be imputed have some special relationship such as that of an employer and employee or that of partners in a partnership. If I send Otto out to purchase some dynamite for blasting gopher holes and he negligently becomes involved in a fender bender with our postman (who was driving his truck and trying to read the paper at the same time), then my attempt to sue the postman for negligence would permit the postman to impute Otto's contributory negligence to me because we have an employer-employee relationship.

A few states have discarded the notion of contributory negligence altogether in favor of comparative negligence. In comparative negligence jurisdictions, the jury will apportion the blame when more than one party is at fault. If the accident caused by the negligence of the postman and Otto resulted in damages of $2,000, then the finding by a jury that Otto's negligence was responsible for 25 percent of the damages and the postman's negligence was responsible for the remaining 75 percent of the damages would obligate Otto (or me) to pay $500 to the postman. The postman would be responsible for paying the other $1,500 to Otto. In pure comparative negligence states, a contributorily negligent plaintiff would be able to recover regardless of whether his negligence accounted for 25 percent or 75 percent of the damages. In restricted comparative negligence states, a contributorily negligent plaintiff whose negligence accounts for more than half of the damages would be barred from recovering anything from the defendant.

The other defense that may be raised by a defendant in a negligence action is that the plaintiff voluntarily assumed the risk that resulted in his injuries. It is not necessary that the plaintiff declare to a crowd that he has chosen to assume some risk because it may be implied from his actions. Regardless of whether the assumption of risk is express or implied, however, the plaintiff must have understood the particular risk and then voluntarily chosen to assume it. If I have recently taken up the sport of archery and ask you to balance an apple on your head so that I might reprise the role of William Tell, the fact that you know I am a lousy shot coupled with your choosing of your own free will to place the apple on your head should enable me to defeat any subsequent negligence claims filed by you if my arrow happens to hit you in the leg. The result would be different if I had fraudulently declared to you that I was a professional archer who routinely shot apples off the heads of bratty children when in fact I was unable to hit the side of a barn even while standing inside it. In this case, you could not be said to have knowingly assumed the risk of having me shoot the apple off your head. You agreed to be a target because I held myself out as an expert shot who missed only when he had a relative in his cross-sight.

The plaintiff's decision to assume the risk must be voluntary as well as knowing. My threat to send you to live with Aunt Agatha for the summer if you failed to put the apple on your head would cause your compliance to be characterized as involuntary. You were forced to serve as my target due to your unwillingness to be suffocated by the flowery odors pervading Aunt Agatha's home. Although coercion is a useful tool for helping indecisive people make snap decisions, it will invalidate any attempt by me to raise the assumption of risk defense to defeat your claim that I was negligent.

A person may also expressly assume the risk of injury by signing an agreement that provides for it. If we signed an agreement in which you promised to balance an apple on your head in exchange for my paying you $1,000 and you agreed to assume any risks of injury that might result, then such an agreement would probably be enforceable and I could raise it as a defense if you later sued me for negligence after shooting an arrow into your shoulder. Absent fraud or coercion, I would probably be able to prevail in any negligence action filed by you because of your agreement to assume the risk that I might hit you with an arrow.

CHAPTER 4

Strict Liability and Product Liability

Men at some times are masters of their fates;
The fault, dear Brutus, is not in our stars,
But in ourselves, that we are underlings.

— William Shakespeare

4

Strict Liability

We saw in the previous chapter that a plaintiff seeking to recover damages for negligence must demonstrate that the defendant breached his duty of care thereby causing the plaintiff to suffer an injury. Although our society imposes an affirmative duty on every person to conduct himself in a manner that does not create an undue risk of harm to others, there are certain dangerous activities for which an injured plaintiff will be able to recover damages without having to demonstrate that a duty of care was breached. Consequently, we will hold the individual who engages in blasting activities, for example, strictly liable for any harm his hobby causes to any other persons. The fact that the blasting enthusiast took as many precautions as was humanly possible will not be considered because he is absolutely liable for the damages caused by such activities.

A plaintiff seeking to establish that she is entitled to recover damages from a defendant engaged in those

activities for which strict liability is imposed will
have to demonstrate that (1) the defendant had an
absolute duty to conduct those activities in a safe
manner (2) but that the defendant breached that duty
(3) and his breach was an actual and proximate cause
of the personal injury or property damage suffered
by the plaintiff. The appropriateness of a strict liability claim will necessarily depend on whether the
factual situation can be characterized as involving
activities that are inherently dangerous or that fit
into one of several less obvious categories.

People who keep wild animals such as lions, tigers,
and bears are absolutely liable for any injuries that
their animals inflict on other persons even though
the mauling may have appeared "playful." Such animals are considered to be inherently dangerous owing to their sharp teeth and claws as well as their
unpredictable dispositions. The fact that a wild animal may have been domesticated to some extent will
not make any difference if the animal is of a type
that could pose a danger to humans owing to its physical characteristics. If I keep a lion on my property
and I poke it with a stick on occasion to keep its man-
eating instincts honed, I will be strictly liable for any
injuries caused by the lion to another person. My
attempt to obscure the true identity of my beast by
attaching a long tail, a pointed nose, and two round
ears to his body to pass him off as a giant mouse will
not enable me to argue successfully that I should not
be liable for the injuries he causes. Although mice
are not animals for which strict liability is imposed
on their owners, one cannot disguise a dangerous

animal as an innocuous animal (albeit an oversized
one) and thus avoid liability for the injuries caused
by the animal.

The owner of an animal that we would not automatically characterize as a potential killer such as
a dog or a cat is not strictly liable for injuries caused
by the animal unless he knows that the animal has
dangerous propensities. Because one cannot know
about the vicious tendencies of one's white rabbit, for
example, until the white rabbit decapitates the milkman and drags his body into a burrow, such animals
are entitled to one free bite so that the owner may
learn of its violent behavior and take the appropriate
precautions. Although the owner of the white rabbit
would undoubtedly feel very bad about the milkman
being dragged into the rabbit hole, the representative
of the milkman's estate would have to demonstrate
that the owner had some knowledge of the rabbit's
vicious temperament before the owner could be held
strictly liable. If the rabbit had been a warm cuddly
little creature until the milkman made the mistake
of patting his head and calling him "honey bunny,"
then the owner could not be said to have been aware
of the boiling cauldron of rage beneath the furry fluff
of his pet.

The imposition of strict liability for injuries inflicted by the landowner's animals will also depend
on the legal status of the person venturing onto the
landowner's property. If the visitor is an invitee or
a licensee and has his arm ripped off by a ferocious
rabbit, then the visitor would be entitled to draw
what is left of his body to its full height and demand

that the landowner get him a bandage for his wound because the landowner would be strictly liable for any injuries caused by the rabbit. If the visitor was a trespasser, by contrast, then the landowner would not be strictly liable for the injuries caused by the rabbit; the trespasser will be able to recover damages from the landowner only if the landowner failed to notify the discovered trespasser of the danger posed by the rabbit. The landowner would not incur liability for negligence if he failed to warn an undiscovered trespasser about the rabbit.

A landowner will also be strictly liable for any injuries resulting from his engaging in abnormally dangerous activities regardless of the degree of care he exercises. These activities are often so dangerous that they cannot be carried out in complete safety regardless of the protective measures taken by the operator. Moreover, these activities are not carried out in heavily populated areas very frequently owing to their ultrahazardous nature. Some of the more common examples of such activities include blasting, manufacturing explosives, oil drilling, and coal mining. Although the particular type of activity is probably most important in deciding whether to characterize it as being abnormally dangerous, the actual location of the activity may also affect the type of liability imposed on the landowner. If I start blasting operations next to a hospital for pea-brained wealthy people, then I will be strictly liable for any injuries caused to the patients and staff by the blasts. However, if I conduct my blasting operations out in the middle of a vast wasteland where the only signs of life are scraggly clumps of vegetation and a few disoriented tour guides, then my activities might not result in the imposition of strict liability owing to the desolation of the landscape. In most cases, however, the inherently dangerous nature of the activity—not the location where it is carried out—will determine whether the owner will be strictly liable for any injuries caused by the activity.

As with simple negligence actions, the defendant's activities must be a proximate as well as an actual cause of the plaintiff's injuries. Even though I might be exploding huge bombs on my property because I wish to create a replica of the Grand Canyon, your ability to recover damages from me will depend on whether you can demonstrate that my excavation activities caused a book to fall off a shelf and onto your head even though you were some fifteen miles away from the blast site. In such a situation, you would have to establish a direct causal relationship between my blasting activities and your head injury as well as show that there were no intervening events that would have severed the causal connection. If your next-door neighbor was digging a large hole for a swimming pool, then I would probably be able to defeat your attempt to recover damages from me because it would be more likely that your neighbor would have been responsible for the vibrations rocking your house.

Workers' compensation programs impose strict liability on an employer for any injuries suffered by its employees while they are working on behalf of their employer. Although some classes of workers such as agricultural laborers and domestic servants (such as Aunt Agatha's staff) are exempt from workers' compensation statutes and are left to pursue any common law remedies they may have against their employer, most office and factory workers are covered by these statutes. Consequently, the employer of such workers will be liable for any injuries these workers incur while working within the scope of their employment regardless of the number of precautions taken by the employer. The workers' compensation laws would apply to Edward Nail, the proprietor of The Nail Factory, one of the world's largest manufacturers of nails, even if he suddenly underwent a spiritual conversion and actually began to care about the lives of his employees. If the "new" Edward began manufacturing only foam rubber nails so that his employees would run less risk of cutting their fingers, Edward would still be liable for any injuries suffered by his employees while at work. Although one would have to be very clumsy to get injured by a foam rubber nail, Edward would still have to pay the injured employee for any necessary medical treatment as well as a certain percentage of his wages for the time the employee is unable to work. An employee who suffered the loss of a limb, for example, would also be covered by the workers' compensation program, and the amount paid for such a loss would likely be determined by a specific state statute.

Although an employer such as Edward Nail must purchase insurance to provide the necessary medical coverage for his employees, he cannot be sued for negligence by a disgruntled employee who believes that the workers' compensation awards are too low because workers' compensation laws automatically bar the use by the injured employee of any common law remedies. The employer will be able to prevent recovery by the injured employee only if the employee intentionally injured herself (by stapling her foot to the floor so that she would not have to go to the monthly worker hygiene meeting) or suffered injury while trying to harm another employee (such as the one who was to give a lecture about foot fungus at the hygiene meeting).

Product Liability

The term *product liability* does not refer to a particular theory of liability applicable to those who negligently design, manufacture, or sell defective products. Instead it is an umbrella term that refers to several different theories under which an injured plaintiff may proceed against the seller or manufacturer of an unreasonably dangerous product. These product liability theories include negligence, strict tort liability, misrepresentations, express warranties, and implied warranties of merchantability and fitness for a particular purpose. Because the world is full of people who wish to foist their defective goods on the general public, the potential litigant must be aware of the elements in each of these causes of action as well as the advantages and disadvantages of each approach.

Negligence

The enterprising products liability plaintiff may wish to begin with negligence because a cause of action based on the negligent design or manufacture of a product is really no different than any other negligence action. The plaintiff must demonstrate that he was owed a duty of care by the defendant and that the defendant's breach of that duty of care was an actual cause and a proximate cause of the damages suffered by the plaintiff. The fact that the plaintiff may be a remote party who did not actually acquire the defective product from the entity responsible for its defects will not defeat the plaintiff's claim because one does not need to be in privity (have a contractual relationship) with the defendant to maintain an action for negligence. Not requiring the plaintiff and defendant to be in privity with each other gives manufacturers and distributors a greater incentive to try to minimize the risks that unreasonably dangerous products will be sold to the public (by making more thorough inspections as well as improving the product's design and manufacture) because anyone who acquires the product—not just the original purchaser—can bring suit for negligence. Hence, the focus will be on any party who could foreseeably be injured by the product—not just the original purchaser of the product.

The plaintiff must establish that she was owed a duty of care by the manufacturer or the distributor of the defective product and that the duty of care was breached. As with standard negligence cases, the defendant's conduct will be evaluated by asking whether its behavior was reasonable under the circumstances. Was it reasonable for the candy company to stick razor-sharp needles in its toffee? Was it reasonable for the automobile manufacturer to leave the brakes off the stripped-down version of its compact car? The factual circumstances will determine whether the defendant acted in an appropriate manner.

A product might be found to be defectively designed if each unit of that product posed an unreasonable danger to the user owing to its particular mechanical design. To establish that the manufacturer should be held liable, however, the plaintiff must demonstrate that an ordinary manufacturer in that industry could have determined that the defective design posed a danger to the product's users before the product was actually sold to consumers. The plaintiff would not be able to succeed in a design defect claim if the average manufacturer was not able to determine that the defect posed a danger to the product's users until after the product itself was actually marketed. If I sold eyebrow bleach to the public and my product was found to cause symptoms in its users ranging from orange teeth to gender confusion, any disgruntled consumer suing me for my defective formulation of the product would succeed in a claim of negligence only if he could show that I somehow knew of these symptoms before the product was actually distributed to the public. I, on the other hand, would want to show that I had tested the product extensively prior to it being marketed in department stores and that these tests revealed nothing that hinted at its many side effects. My success in demonstrating that a typical cosmetics manufacturer could not have known prior to the marketing of my product that it would cause the above-referenced symptoms would enable me to defeat a claim for negligence.

The plaintiff wishing to establish that a product was designed in a defective manner may be required to show that the manufacturer could have designed the product in a way that would have reduced the risks of injury associated with using it. However, the fact that my eyebrow bleach could have been made safer is not in itself determinative of whether my product was formulated in a negligent manner. If the eyebrow bleach could have been made safer only by adding a rare and expensive mineral found in black coral caves in the South China Sea, my failure to add such a precious ingredient would not in itself constitute negligence because such an ingredient would make my product prohibitively expensive to manufacture. A finding of negligence would also depend on whether it was reasonable for consumers to expect that my eyebrow bleach would have no side effects. If my product was the latest in a long line of eyebrow bleaches causing symptoms ranging from cramps to freckling, then my product would likely arouse no great expectations on the part of consumers that it would be without side effects. Consequently, a jury hearing a negligence claim against me might find that my product was no better and no worse than its many competitors so that my product could not be regarded as having been negligently designed. After all, there would be no completely benign eyebrow bleach against which my particular product could be compared.

A manufacturing defect, by contrast, occurs when a particular unit in a product line is manufactured in a way that causes it to pose an unforeseeable risk of injury to the user. If my eyebrow bleach contains several active ingredients including battery acid that are emptied into individual bottles as the bottles move along a conveyor belt, then a malfunction in the battery acid dispenser that causes it to add ten times the normal amount of battery acid to a bottle of my eyebrow bleach would be considered a manufacturing defect. The lucky soul who purchased that "enhanced" bottle of eyebrow bleach would not only enjoy the questionable sensation of having her eyebrows "go nuclear" but would also be able to file suit against me for my negligent manufacture of my product. The plaintiff might also rely on the doctrine of *res ipsa loquitur* to bolster her negligence claim against me because it is unlikely that the product could have been manufactured in such a way without my having been negligent.

What sort of duty is owed to the consumer by the distributor of a negligently designed or manufactured product? Although wholesalers and retailers owe a duty of care to those persons who could foreseeably suffer injury from such products, these parties will not generally have a duty to make anything more than a casual inspection of the products unless they have some reason to believe that a more detailed examination is necessary. If the retailer or wholesaler has purchased its supplies from a reputable manufacturer, then it would not be obliged to make a detailed inspection of all items before selling them to either another distributor or the general public unless it had some reason to believe that the goods might be unreasonably dangerous. The manufacturer, by contrast, will usually be required to inspect and test samplings of its products; it will not be able to avoid liability arising from its failure to conduct such inspections by contracting these duties out to another party.

The extent to which a manufacturer has a duty to warn the public of the risks of using its product will depend on the extent to which the danger is obvious to someone purchasing the product as well as the relative expense of making the product safe (as opposed to putting a warning label on it). If I sell sharp knives to homemakers who are interested in getting more out of their marriages, I would not be required to put a warning label on the knife or somehow design a device that makes it impossible for the consumers to injure themselves with it because the danger posed by the knife is obvious. Any person of average intelligence would know that a knife is to be used for slicing things and not for some other purpose such as calligraphy. The risk posed by eyebrow bleach, by contrast, would not be so obvious to a consumer even if that consumer had tried a number of other eyebrow bleaches and suffered various burns, abrasions, and emotional trauma. If my eyebrow bleach caused the usual assortment of dermatological injuries, I would be required to put a label on each bottle warning of any potential side effects. If a minimal investment would make it possible to manufacture the product so that it was still effective but did not have the undesirable side effects, then my failure to make this investment might be regarded as a breach of my duty of care. If there is no known way of eliminating the side effects associated with this product, however, then I would probably be able to satisfy my duty of care to the consumer by putting warning labels on the bottles. If I could show that my only duty of care was to warn the consumer of the possible consequences of using the eyebrow bleach (which I satisfied by pasting brightly colored warning labels on the bottles), then I would probably be able to defeat a consumer's claim of negligence because he was put on notice of the risks and still used the product.

As with the standard negligence action, a consumer (who is able to demonstrate that I did not adequately warn her of the dangers of using the eyebrow bleach or that I failed to make the product safer when it was feasible for me to do so) will still have to show that the product itself was both an actual cause as well as a proximate cause of her injuries. In short, the plaintiff must show that she would not have suffered her injuries but for her use of my eyebrow bleach. In addition, she must prove that there was a direct causal connection between her use of my product and her injuries. If the consumer suffered from a rare disease that caused her face to burst into flame on a regular basis, then this physical characteristic would weaken her argument that it was the eyebrow bleach that caused her eyebrows to catch fire.

One example of an unforeseeable intervening cause would be if a psychopathic baker had burst into the plaintiff's bedroom (immediately after the plaintiff had applied the eyebrow bleach) and tossed a birthday cake with lit candles at the plaintiff thus causing her eyebrows to catch fire. I might be able to argue successfully that the burns were caused by the lit candles instead of the eyebrow bleach and thus show that any causal connection between the eyebrow bleach and the burns was indirect at best.

Because product design defects originate with the manufacturer and cannot be attributed to other parties in the distribution network such as wholesalers or retailers, the manufacturer will be liable for any injuries that are caused by the design defect. As far as defects in the manufacturing of the product itself are concerned, the plaintiff will have to demonstrate that the flaw in the product existed at the time the manufacturer transferred it to a wholesaler, retailer, or some other party. If the plaintiff is unable to prove that the flaw in the product existed at the time a wholesaler or retailer acquired it, then the manufacturer will not be held liable for the defect. If the plaintiff wishes to try his luck in court with the distributors, he will have to demonstrate either that the particular wholesaler or retailer acted in a negligent manner (by mislabeling toxic chemicals with eyebrow bleach labels) or that it failed to inspect the product when it had reason to believe that the product might be defective. The fact that many customers with severe burns were returning their eyebrow bleach bottles to the cosmetics counter at the local department store would give the owners of that store sufficient reason to investigate whether the eyebrow bleach should be pulled from the shelves. If the owners decided not to investigate the eyebrow bleach despite the complaints of many dissatisfied and disfigured customers, then they would probably be found liable for failing to exercise their duty of care with the plaintiffs. Once a retailer, for example, is given notice that one of its products poses an unreasonable risk to its customers, then it is obligated to investigate the truth of these complaints. It cannot avoid this responsibility by arguing that the manufacturer or wholesaler who sold it the product should be solely liable even though it failed to inspect the product.

Strict Tort Liability

If a plaintiff is injured by a defective product that poses an unreasonable risk to its user regardless of how many precautions are taken by the manufacturer, then the plaintiff may choose to sue the manufacturer or distributor based on a theory of strict tort liability. To maintain an action based on strict tort liability, the plaintiff must demonstrate that she was owed an absolute duty of care by a commercial seller, which the seller breached, and that such breach was both an actual cause and a proximate cause of the injuries suffered by the plaintiff. Whether the defect in the product was a design flaw or a manufacturing flaw is not important so long as the defect made the product unreasonably dangerous.

Claims for damages under a theory of strict tort liability may be brought only against commercial enterprises and not private citizens who occasionally sell unreasonably dangerous items. Moreover, one will usually be limited to proceeding against a seller of goods or goods and services as opposed to those persons who merely sell services (such as sidewalk hostesses) because the latter may be sued using a simple negligence theory. Consequently, the plaintiff who is injured by a vacuum cleaner that burst into flame when it was activated may proceed against its manufacturer, the Gyro Vacuum Cleaner Company. Although the company is owned by Vic Gyro, a somewhat unstable fellow, who believes that combustible appliances are simply one of the hazards of living in a modern technological society, the plaintiff should be able to demonstrate that a flaming vacuum cleaner poses an unreasonable risk of injury to the user and that the manufacturer should be held strictly liable.

As noted previously, the finding that a product is defective depends primarily on how severely its performance departs from what is expected by the consumer. If all vacuum cleaners were designed to burst into flame when activated, then the defendant might be able to argue that the plaintiff should have taken the appropriate precautions (such as putting on a fireproof suit) before using the vacuum cleaner. Because most people do not expect their household appliances to explode when they switch them on, the plaintiff can argue that he was unable to take the necessary safety precautions because he had no expectation that he would be engulfed by flames.

Although the plaintiff does not need to be in privity with the Gyro Vacuum Cleaner Company to maintain an action for strict tort liability against it, the success of his claim would depend in part on whether the vacuum cleaner was significantly altered by a wholesaler or retailer before it was purchased by the plaintiff. If the retailer, Aaron Airbag, fancied himself to be something of an electrician and he rewired the vacuum cleaner thus transforming it from a perfectly safe household appliance into an electrical torch, then the plaintiff's claim against the manufacturer would be dismissed. It was the incompetent rewiring of the vacuum cleaner by the retailer—not a design or manufacturing flaw—that was responsible for the plaintiff's burns.

The plaintiff must prove only that the product was unreasonably dangerous in order to establish that the seller breached its duty of care. As with an action for negligence, this step may be accomplished by showing that the manufacturer failed to give sufficient warning to the consumer (if there was no feasible way of making the product safer) or that the manufacturer failed to make the product safe when that task could have been accomplished without making relatively significant expenditures. If vacuum cleaner technology was very primitive and there was no feasible way to make them safer, then the defendant might be able to avoid liability if it plastered its products with prominent warning labels.

To show that the product defect was both an actual cause and a proximate cause of his injuries, the plaintiff must demonstrate that the product was defective when it was sold or otherwise transferred by the defendant to the plaintiff. If the issue is whether adequate warnings were given of the risks of injury associated with using the product, then the plaintiff must show that he would not have been injured but for the defendant's failure to inform the plaintiff of those risks. As with negligence actions, the plaintiff can recover only for personal injuries or property damages that he has personally suffered. As demonstrated by the newsstand example, one who suffers a purely economic loss such as lost wages will be unable to recover damages.

Although the defendant may avoid liability if the danger posed by its product is obvious as would be the case with the manufacturer of cutlery, there are also a number of other defenses that may be employed by either a manufacturer or distributor of a product to defeat a strict liability claim. If I purchased a vacuum cleaner from the Gyro Vacuum Cleaner Company but decided to use it to cut my grass and the clippings caused the motor to catch fire (which resulted in my being injured), then my misuse of the product would provide both the manufacturer and the distributor with a viable defense to my claim. Although it might be reasonable for vacuum cleaner sellers to anticipate that I might use the vacuum cleaner to vacuum the grease-covered floor of my garage as well as my rugs, it is not reasonable for them to expect that I would use a vacuum cleaner to manicure my lawn. Consequently, I would probably be unable to recover any damages regardless of the severity of my injuries because the vacuum cleaner caught fire due to my misuse of it and not any inherent defect in the product itself.

Chapter 4

A manufacturer may also be able to avoid strict tort liability for injuries caused by its products if the injuries could not be anticipated prior to the product being distributed to the public. If I began manufacturing an innocuous brand of eyebrow bleach without the pyrotechnic characteristics of my earlier formulations, the fact that this eyebrow bleach causes the user's nose to shift upward over time will not render me strictly liable if there was no way for me to detect this side effect prior to my making the decision to market it to the public. The fact that my product may cause a user's nose to shift to the top of his head after several years of steady use would arguably lend credence to his belief that my product is unreasonably dangerous, but I should not be held responsible for consequences that were impossible for me to anticipate or otherwise detect by repeated testings of the product. My defense would be bolstered if this particular symptom manifested only in a very small number of people such as agoraphobic trapeeze artists and claustrophobic sewer workers.

Contributory negligence and assumption of risk defenses may also be raised by the defendant to defeat strict tort liability. Neither argument will provide the defendant with a viable defense, however, unless the plaintiff understood fully the risk of using the product in a particular manner and acted unreasonably in choosing to use the product in that way. If I purchase a vacuum cleaner from the Gyro Vacuum Cleaner Company that is covered with large stickers warning that the user will be burned if she tries vacuuming her rug with the appliance without wearing a fireproof suit (which can be obtained from the company for an additional charge) and I read and fully understand the warnings but choose to go ahead and turn on the switch, then most people would regard my behavior as unreasonable. Even though many people who like to set themselves on fire would think that I acted in a perfectly acceptable manner, the appropriateness of my behavior will be determined by reference to what the average person—not a tiny group of masochistic pyromaniacs—believes is reasonable. Even though I might be the type of person who enjoys getting a good sunburn, my behavior would not be regarded as prudent by even the most ardent sun worshipper.

Misrepresentations

A plaintiff hoping to place a crown of thorns on the head of the manufacturer or distributor of a defective product could claim that he was injured because he relied on a material misstatement of fact made by the seller about the product. However, the plaintiff would have to demonstrate that the misrepresentation of fact did cause him to purchase the product and that his injuries were caused by his reliance on that misrepresentation. If I offer to sell my Aunt Agatha a crowbar for changing tires and picking her teeth after formal dinners, my statement that the crowbar is made of an extremely light strategic metal that will not chip or crack under the most extreme conditions might induce her to buy my crowbar instead of going down the street to Ye Olde Crowbar Shoppe. If my crowbar is actually a hollow tube of plastic covered with a sheet of tin, then my statement would constitute a misrepresentation of fact because the crowbar is not made of a lightweight strategic metal. This fact would become painfully clear the next time Aunt Agatha's limousine got a flat tire and her newly hired chauffeur, Driver Bob, splintered the crowbar while trying to pry the hubcap off the deflated tire. Assuming that the splinters damaged the finish of the limousine as well as scratched the face and hands of Driver Bob, then both Aunt Agatha and Driver Bob would be able to sue me for misrepresentation because both of them relied on my statement regarding the durability of the crowbar. Moreover, Aunt Agatha could argue that she would have never purchased the plastic crowbar from me if I had told her the truth about its flimsiness.

There are many statements that are not exactly true but are so vague that they cannot be considered misrepresentations of fact. The flowery statements used by a salesman to describe an appliance as "the finest oven money can buy" is regarded as "puffing" instead of a factual misrepresentation because the use of undefined words such as *finest, greatest,* and *best* do not provide an objective standard whereby the accuracy of the statement can be assessed. Such statements are too general to be considered representations regarding particular facts and thus are not actionable. The result will change, however, once statements of facts are introduced into the sales pitch. If an appliance salesman states that the prospective buyer can burn a Thanksgiving turkey in his oven using only half the power of any other existing oven, then the salesman has made a statement that can be verified by comparing cooking times among various ovens. If the statement is false but it induces the buyer to purchase the oven, then the buyer can maintain an action for misrepresentation. Because the salesman will necessarily present himself as an expert on appliances, he will be given less freedom to make "puffing" statements than a private individual who is trying to sell an unwanted oven that he received as a wedding gift. The latter person does not sell appliances for a living and would not be considered an expert for purposes of assessing liability for borderline misrepresentations of fact.

The plaintiff seeking to recover damages for misrepresentation must show that the defendant intended that the plaintiff rely on his misstatement of fact and that the plaintiff did in fact so rely. The fact that the salesman declares that the oven is self-cleaning and can be used to wash clothing would probably be regarded as evidence of his intent to induce reliance by the customer. Because we cannot read the minds of people and thus determine what they are really thinking, we must look to their statements and actions to draw conclusions about their intentions. The plaintiff must then show that she justifiably relied on the statement in deciding to purchase the oven. If the plaintiff laughed in disbelief at the salesman's statement about washing clothes in the oven but went ahead and purchased the appliance, she would not be able to maintain an action for misrepresentation against the salesman because that statement did not cause the plaintiff to purchase the oven. However, a contrary outcome could result if the misrepresentation was a significant (but not solitary) factor in the plaintiff's decision to purchase the oven.

The plaintiff must also demonstrate that the misrepresentation was both an actual cause and a proximate cause of his damages and that there are no countervailing defenses. As with strict tort liability actions, the defendant may raise either the assumption of risk by or contributory negligence of the plaintiff as a defense to liability. The assumption of risk defense will defeat a cause of action only if the plaintiff was not entitled to rely on the misrepresentation of fact. If I go into a store to buy a tire and the salesman hands me a ceramic plate and declares that it is a tire, my decision to go ahead with the purchase even though any fool could see that I was purchasing a plate instead of a tire would not constitute justifiable reliance. If I later became involved in an accident when the ceramic plate on the right rear axle of my car shattered, my action for misrepresentation would probably be thrown out of court because my reliance on the salesman's statement that I was purchasing a tire was not justifiable. The fact that I am something of a moron when it comes to automobiles will not help my legal position. As far as contributory negligence is concerned, however, it may be raised only if the misrepresentation of fact was negligent; the defendant who makes an intentional misrepresentation of fact will not be permitted to raise the defense of the plaintiff's contributory negligence.

Chapter 4

Express Warranties

Express warranties are similar to misrepresentations of fact. Both involve affirmative statements (either oral or written) regarding a product on which a consumer may rely in deciding to purchase that product. An express warranty is a statement of fact or a promise that induces the buyer to purchase a particular item. Unlike misrepresentations of fact, however, anyone selling the product—not just a commercial vendor—may be liable for breaching an express warranty. The potential class of plaintiffs may also be larger when express warranties are involved. We saw previously that only those persons who justifiably relied on the specific misrepresentation of fact will be able to recover damages from the defendant. However, those persons who are entitled to maintain an action against a defendant for breach of an express warranty only need to be members of any one of the following three groups: (1) the buyer of the product and any other members of the buyer's family as well as her houseguests who suffer personal injuries; (2) any person who could be expected to use or consume the product who suffers personal injuries; or (3) any legal entity (such as a corporation or partnership) or natural person who could be expected to use or consume the product who suffers personal injury or property damage.

Although the first alternative is the most restricted class of potential plaintiffs, it is also the most widely adopted because many states are reluctant to impose liability for the breach of an express warranty when the person claiming the injury has no relationship to either the seller or the buyer. We can see how some potential plaintiffs might be prevented from maintaining a suit for the breach of an express warranty if the state in which they live has adopted the first alternative. If I sell new and improved eyebrow bleach to you and state that it not only will give you platinum eyebrows but also will not have any of the side effects associated with other brands of eyebrow bleach on the market, you could sue me for the breach of that warranty if your cousin Heather (who is visiting your home) applies the eyebrow bleach and suffers severe burns. Heather is within the class of potential plaintiffs described in the first alternative. What happens if Heather throws the bottle away but it is subsequently pulled out of the trash can by Queen Victoria, who has always wanted to lighten her eyebrows? Queen Victoria will not be able to recover damages against me under the first alternative because she is not a member of your family or your houseguest. Her recovery under the second alternative depends on whether the jury hearing her case decides that it was foreseeable that someone such as a British monarch would pull the bottle out of the trash can and apply the eyebrow bleach. If Queen Victoria was delighted with the product but accidentally spilled some eyebrow bleach on her robe and discolored it (despite a label on the bottle that said the eyebrow bleach would not harm fabrics), then she would be able to recover damages only under the third alternative because that is the only one that permits plaintiffs to recover for property damages caused by a breach of express warranty.

Chapter 4

As with the other product liability theories, contributory negligence and the assumption of risk will provide defenses to a claim that an express warranty has been breached. The defendant may also raise the defense that the plaintiff failed to give notice of the breach within a reasonable period of time. If you purchase a rubber face mask at a costume store for Halloween only because the salesman assured you that there was no chance that a human body part could have been erroneously put into the box, then your decision to go ahead and purchase the boxed mask would be based in part on the salesman's promise that you were purchasing a rubber mask.

If you do not open the box until you get it home and you then find, much to your horror, that you have acquired the missing head of my late Uncle Buster, then your failure to inform the seller within a reasonable time that your realistic-looking mask is actually a real head may prevent you from recovering any damages from the seller. If you decide that Uncle Buster's head would look very nice on the mantle next to the family portrait and you keep it there for several months, then you might be estopped from demanding that the seller take the head back and refund your money. Moreover, the passage of time would weaken any presumption in your favor that you had suffered severe emotional trauma when you opened the box and found my Uncle Buster staring back at you. In any event, one should always try to return merchandise that does not measure up to the standards of the promises made by the salesman as quickly as possible.

What if the costume shop has a disclaimer on the box stating that "the seller makes no warranties regarding the nature of the goods or materials contained in this box"? Would such a broad disclaimer enable the seller to avoid refunding your money if you decided to bring Uncle Buster back to the store? In general, the answer is negative because the seller gave an express warranty regarding the contents of the box by his statements as well as his handing you a box covered with pictures of the rubber mask and words describing the product that you thought you were purchasing. Disclaimers will usually be upheld only when they clarify the express warranty in some way. If the box actually contained a rubber mask but the print on the side stated that "this mask is made of the finest latex rubber but it will tear if it is subjected to extreme heat or cold," then the disclaimer would clarify any express warranties regarding the durability of the rubber mask.

Implied Warranties

The final path available to an aggrieved plaintiff who wishes to seek redress for any personal injuries caused by a defective product is to claim that the seller breached an implied warranty that the product was merchantable or that it was fit for a particular purpose. The implied warranty of merchantability means that the goods sold by a merchant are of average quality and are fit for the purposes for which they are generally used. A butcher who sells you rancid steaks will have breached the implied warranty of merchantability because the steaks are not of average quality and are not fit for human consumption. Consequently, the butcher will have breached this implied warranty by virtue of her sale to you of the rancid meat regardless of whether she ever made express statements about the quality of the steaks.

The implied warranty of fitness for a particular purpose arises in situations where the buyer relies on the special skills or knowledge of the seller and has informed the seller of his purpose for purchasing the goods. If I explain to a salesman at Garden World that I need to buy some fertilizer for my garden and he suggests that I buy a five-gallon container of asphalt and spread it on my flowerbed to give the flowers those extra petroleum-based nutrients not usually found in most plant fertilizers, then my subsequent purchase and use of the asphalt in my flowerbed would give me the right to file a suit against the salesman and Garden World if the asphalt killed all my flowers. The salesman and his employer would not have been liable had they sold me the asphalt without making any affirmations regarding its utility as a fertilizer because I would then only be able to maintain a cause of action if the asphalt was of substandard quality. It is the affirmative statement by the salesman that the asphalt may be used to fertilize flowers that causes an implied warranty of fitness for a particular purpose to be inferred.

As far as the defendants are concerned, only a merchant who deals in the particular good that is alleged to be substandard can be held responsible for breaching an implied warranty of merchantability. A butcher sells meat for a living and may be held responsible

for breaching an implied warranty of merchantability if she sells rancid meat. If I buy steaks from an
enterprising fellow on a streetcorner who has several
bags of meat for sale, then I will probably be unable
to assert that the rancid meat I purchased from him
was implicitly warranted to be merchantable because
the streetcorner meat peddler is obviously not a
butcher. It is more likely that he is a casual seller
who is having a one-time sale. By way of contrast,
one does not have to be a merchant of the particular
goods being sold to be presumed to have given an
implied warranty of fitness for a particular purpose
so long as the seller knew of the buyer's need and
possessed some special skill or knowledge on which
the buyer relied in making her purchase. Although
the Garden World salesman would be presumed to
have given an implied warranty of fitness for a particular purpose when he sold me the asphalt for my
flowers, the same sort of implicit warranty might be
imposed on a professor of hydrocarbon chemistry who
brews asphalt in her basement and declares it to be
the best flower fertilizer in the world. My explaining
my fertilizer need to the professor coupled with her
special knowledge about hydrocarbons and petro-
leum products in general will result in her being
charged with having given me an implied warranty
of fitness for a particular purpose if I purchase asphalt from her for my garden. The fact that the professor makes asphalt as a hobby and sells it to the
public only on religious holidays would not affect her
liability because one does not have to be a merchant
to give this warranty.

A defendant seeking to defeat the application of either of these implied warranties may argue that the plaintiff knowingly assumed the risk that the implied warranty of merchantability was breached as would be the case if I decided to go ahead and eat the rancid meat to see if I could develop a taste for spoiled food. The defendant could also argue that I was contributorily negligent in consuming the meat after discovering that it was rancid. However, I would not be contributorily negligent if I stopped eating the meat once I discovered that it was spoiled. In any event, I would want to notify the seller of his breach of the implied warranty within a reasonable time or else I might find myself unable to recover damages for any personal injuries or property damages I incurred by using or otherwise consuming the defective goods.

CHAPTER 5

Other Torts

The liberty of the individual must be thus far limited; he must not make himself a nuisance to other people.

— John Stuart Mill

5

Nuisances

We all have very strong views about the things that annoy us, such as door-to-door salesmen, presidential news conferences, and actors-turned-bestselling-authors, and we would probably not hesitate to characterize many of these things as nuisances. Yet we might be hard-pressed to define what it is about these things that makes them nuisances. We would also be surprised to find that the legal concept of nuisance is much more restrictive than the word *nuisance* as it is used by the general public because the former comes into play only when we are discussing the rights of individuals to enjoy the use of their land without unwarranted interference from others.

Being a nuisance is easy because the would-be tortfeasor merely has to act in a way that unreasonably interferes with the right of another party to use or enjoy her land. The tort of nuisance may be distinguished from that of trespass in that the former relates to activities that deprive the party in rightful possession of the land of its lawful right to use and enjoy the land, whereas the latter relates to activities that interfere with that party's exclusive possessory interest in the land. A nuisance does not involve the physical exclusion of a person from her land but instead concerns the extent to which her enjoyment of her land has been impaired. In general, most nuisance cases involve foul odors, excessive noises, or repulsive visual displays that disturb the solitude of neighboring landowners. However, the nuisance must be regarded by a reasonable person as an unwarranted interference with the landowner's right to use and enjoy her property; the fact that a person is extraordinarily sensitive to a particular odor, sound, or sight will not enable her to maintain an action for nuisance if persons of ordinary sensibilities would not be similarly aggravated.

In deciding whether a particular thing constitutes an unreasonable interference with another person's right to use and enjoy his property, one must balance the value of the activity giving rise to the unwanted noise, sound, or sight against the degree of injury suffered by the landowner. This balancing test is employed because every person is entitled to use his property as he sees fit so long as the particular use does not violate the law or otherwise unreasonably infringe on the rights of adjacent landowners. Because we do not wish to allow a person's unfettered use of his land to interfere with the rights of his neighbors, the value of the use must greatly exceed the discomfort suffered by the affected neighbors. If

Chapter 5

I become inspired by a recent best-seller about three little pigs, I might decide to begin raising pigs and go so far as to build a nice mud pen and purchase a dozen fine porcine specimens. Even if my new pets grunted so loudly that they interfered with the radio and television signals received in the homes of my neighbors, I would still be happy with my decision to get into the porcine husbandry business. My enthusiasm for my portly pets would not be dampened even by the overpowering odor emitted by some of my more malodorous beasts even though my neighbors might believe that the local chemical plant was leaking. If one of the other residents on my street, such as Miss Tuttleworth, did not support my efforts to help our country maintain its lead in porcine husbandry technology, she might decide that she had no option but to go to court and obtain an injunction ordering me to stop breeding pigs. The basis of her complaint would be that our stuffy, blue-blooded community is hardly the place for a pig farm and that I should not be permitted to continue pursuing my hobby because its slight commercial utility is far outweighed by the discomfort it causes to my neighbors. Owing to the fact that I had erected the pigpen after my neighbors had built their homes (thus preventing me from arguing that my pigpen should have "grandfather" rights because my neighbors had "come to the nuisance"), Miss Tuttleworth would probably be able to obtain an order requiring me to get rid of my pigs.

One must distinguish between private nuisances and public nuisances. The former involve situations in which the actions of the defendant somehow interfere with the plaintiff's use and enjoyment of his land. The party entitled to possession of the land is the only one who may bring an action for nuisance insofar as it relates to his property. A public nuisance, by contrast, involves something that affects the public as a whole in some way. A chemical dump might be characterized as a public nuisance because it poses a danger to the health and safety of the entire community. An adjacent landowner would be able to recover damages from the owner of the chemical dump only if he could demonstrate that he had suffered "special" damages that were distinguishable from those suffered by the public. If the adjacent landowner could show that the dump had poisoned his water wells, for example, then he could recover damages because he suffered a type of harm different in degree and extent from that suffered by the community as a whole.

The remedies available to the prevailing party in a nuisance action are twofold. Recovery may be had in the form of money damages that are designed to compensate the injured party for the pecuniary losses caused to her by the nuisance. However, one may choose to seek an injunction ordering the defendant to stop the undesirable activity because the nature of the nuisance may make it impossible to put a price tag on the amount of money that should be awarded to the injured party. Unlike the legal remedy of money damages, an injunction is an equitable remedy that may be more appropriate when the nuisance is expected to continue existing into the indefinite future.

Chapter 5

Because an injunction is a fairly drastic remedy, however, it will be imposed only when the legal remedy of money damages is not adequate (as would be the case if the amount necessary to compensate the injured party for his suffering cannot be calculated) and the nuisance itself is not temporary in nature (so that it might require the injured party to file additional legal claims in the future). An injunction will also be granted only if the plaintiff is able to show that the injunction itself will not cause undue hardship to the defendant. Miss Tuttleworth's request for an injunction ordering me to close down my pigpen might be granted by a court because the particular harm suffered by her (poor television and radio reception coupled with the unpleasant odors emitted by my pigs) could be expected to continue so long as I kept my pigs. Moreover, it would be difficult to put a price tag on the injuries suffered by Miss Tuttleworth because one cannot easily calculate the value of clean air or the joy realized from watching one's favorite game show. Similarly, the collective inconvenience caused to my neighbors by my pigpen coupled with the fact that the pigs are my hobby and not my livelihood would probably cause a judge to determine that an injunction would not cause undue hardship to me. Even though I might argue that the pigs are my soul mates and that they are the only ones who have ever appreciated me for myself, it is unlikely that the judge would be dissuaded from issuing the injunction.

An injured party may choose not to pursue her remedies in court until she has first tried to abate the nuisance directly. By contrast, a person seeking to abate a public nuisance such as a chemical dump would be entitled to take corrective measures only if she had suffered special damages.

Economic Torts

Although most torts affect the financial well-being of the injured party in some way, there are a few torts that may be characterized as *economic torts* because they impair the injured party's pecuniary opportunities or commercial relationships. These economic torts, which include disparagement, interference with contractual relations, and interference with prospective economic advantage, are somewhat amorphous. However, these torts are useful "gap-fillers" that may be used when situations arise in which a defendant's behavior does not quite reach the threshold of or otherwise fit within the bounds of one of the other more common torts such as commercial misappropriation or defamation.

Disparagement is a distant relative of defamation because it consists of a false statement of fact by the defendant regarding the pecuniary interests of the plaintiff that is intentionally published by the defendant. I could become a disparager by declaring to a loan officer at Aunt Agatha's bank that my devoted relative lost her entire fortune in a speculative venture to build atomic reactors for household use powered by pellets of uranium and honeybee dung. Such a statement might cause the bank to refuse to loan Aunt Agatha the money she needs to finance the construction of an office building in our town's business district. Because it may take Aunt Agatha some time to arrange adequate financing from another bank, the delay in construction might hinder her ability to interest prospective tenants in her building and also inflate her building costs.

To succeed in her claim for disparagement against me, Aunt Agatha would have to demonstrate that I intentionally made a false statement about her financial well-being to a third party and that my remarks caused her to suffer some sort of pecuniary injury. The fact that my statement complicated her efforts to obtain construction financing thus delaying the completion of her office building and causing her to lose several tenants (who might have otherwise leased space from her if the building had been completed on time) might render me liable for some of the excess costs incurred by Aunt Agatha due to the delay in bank financing. However, Aunt Agatha might find the burden of proof somewhat difficult to meet because it is unlikely that the bank would have relied solely on my statements in deciding to reject Aunt Agatha's loan application; it could also review Aunt Agatha's financial statements to evaluate her creditworthiness. Furthermore, the bank could examine the nature of the project itself. If the downtown area was littered with empty office buildings, then the bank might have denied Aunt Agatha's loan application based on its belief that the proposed building would not be able to attract enough tenants to be commercially viable. Consequently, the bank would not be able to point to my disparaging statements about Aunt Agatha's financial health as the sole reason for its denial of her loan application. If I wished to continue my career in disparagement, however, I would want to remember that the only available defenses are the absolute and limited privileges available to persons accused of defamation. Because disparagement involves a false statement of fact about the plaintiff, truth cannot be a defense to disparagement as it is in cases involving defamation.

The economic tortfeasor who has mastered disparagement may wish to learn how to interfere with the contractual relations of others. This is not a difficult tort to commit because it merely requires that the tortfeasor intentionally act in some way that interferes with the execution or performance of a contract. The defendant need not necessarily make it impossible for the plaintiff to perform his duties under the contract; the defendant's actions need only make it more difficult for the plaintiff to fulfill his duties under the contract or inflate the costs that the plaintiff will incur prior to the performance of the contract.

To return to the pig example, we might imagine a situation in which my neighbors became enamored with my pigs and they all rushed out to buy pigs of their own so that they could get in on the ground floor of the new porcine craze sweeping the land. As the only porcine breeder in my neighborhood, I might wish to prolong my own notoriety by doing whatever I could to make it more difficult for my neighbors to take delivery of their new pets. I could call all the local pig suppliers and tell them that each of my neighbors was being investigated for passing bad checks. Such a strategic move might cause many of the vendors to refuse to sell any pigs to those among my neighbors who could not pay for their merchandise with cashier checks. In any event, my false statements would probably make it more difficult for my neighbors to buy their pigs. Consequently, they could file suit against me for interfering with their contracts because I admittedly had no right to make false statements about their finances to the pig vendors. That they might also have a cause of action for defamation against me would not compel a court to judge my actions any less harshly.

How might I defend my actions? I could sneak out of town under cover of darkness but that sort of behavior would tend to cast a shadow on my declarations of innocence. It would be more prudent to argue that my neighbors' efforts to become porcine entrepreneurs would interfere with some legitimate interest of mine such as a geographical monopoly that had been granted to me for a fee by the local association of pig breeders (whose members had agreed to supply the porcine needs of my neighbors). Because I had already spent a significant amount of money to purchase a geographical franchise that prevented the association from selling pigs to anyone residing within five hundred yards of my home, then my efforts to prevent my neighbors from becoming pig breeders (though not admirable) might be seen as being justified. However, my success in defeating a claim for interference with contractual relations would depend in part on whether my actions were undertaken only after it became clear to me that the members of the association had no intention of abiding by the terms of our franchise agreement.

One can also commit a tortious offense by interfering with the prospective economic advantage of another even when no contract exists. What distinguishes this tort from interference with contractual relations is that the former must be motivated by spite. In other words, my attempt to prevent you from leasing a desirable storefront location for your porcine grooming shop (by informing the leasing agent that you were about to declare bankruptcy even though I had no knowledge of your financial situation) might be considered an unwarranted interference with your prospective economic advantage if my action was motivated solely by my desire to make it impossible for you to open your business. If, on the other hand, I knew for certain that you were about to throw yourself at the feet of a bankruptcy judge and I wanted to protect the interests of the leasing agent (who happened to be my close friend), then I would not be liable for any wrongdoing because my actions were motivated solely by my concern for the welfare of the leasing agent. My statement was not motivated by any desire on my part to deprive you of the location and thus make it more difficult for you to start your business.

Malicious Prosecution and Abuse of Process

The would-be business tycoon may find it necessary to frighten some of her competitors from time to time so that they will be reluctant to challenge her directly in the commercial arena. There is no better way to cower one's adversaries than to have them tossed in jail. The problem with such a strategy is that one may run afoul of the law and incur liability for either malicious prosecution or abuse of process. Although civil libertarians are generally quick to attack the motivations of those business tycoons who try to have their competitors incarcerated, they forget that the world of business is a Darwinian jungle in which only the most resourceful creatures survive.

One can commit the tort of malicious prosecution by intentionally initiating criminal or civil proceedings against the plaintiff without probable cause if the proceedings ultimately terminate in favor of the plaintiff but cause him to suffer damages. The fact that the defendant (initiator) merely tells his story to the prosecutor in a manner that convinces the prosecutor to take action against the plaintiff will not suffice to bring the defendant within the ambit of this tort. The defendant must do something more such as fabricating the evidence that convinces the prosecutor to initiate the proceedings. If I recently stole several rare jeweled eggs from a local museum and I wanted to throw the authorities off my trail, I might hand one or two of the jeweled eggs over to the police and declare that I had found them in your mailbox when I stopped by your house to drop off a piece of mail that had been misdelivered to my home. If I was a credible actor, the police might obtain an arrest warrant and drag you into the station right away so that you could be interrogated as to the whereabouts of the other eggs. Regardless of whether the police found your tear-laden alibi to be convincing, the evidence might still persuade the prosecutor to go ahead with her plan to try you for grand larceny. If you were found innocent of the charge but your reputation was destroyed by the publicity surrounding your alleged theft of the jeweled eggs, then you might choose to bring an action against me for malicious prosecution.

To succeed in your claim of malicious prosecution, you would have to show that my behavior was motivated not by any genuine conviction that you were guilty but instead by my own selfish desire to have you take the blame for the theft of the eggs. Moreover, you would have to demonstrate that I did not have any reason to suspect that you committed the theft. If I confessed while testifying at your trial that I had stolen the eggs, then the court could easily conclude that my efforts to initiate criminal proceedings against you were improperly motivated and taken without any sincere belief on my part that you were actually guilty of the theft. All of this would not do you any good, however, unless the proceedings terminated in your favor. If you were found guilty of stealing the eggs, then you would be unable to file a malicious prosecution claim against me. You would also have to establish that the proceedings caused you to suffer damages. These damages would include the costs you incurred in defending yourself against the charges and the harm caused to your reputation by the trial as well as the humiliation you suffered from being tried as a criminal. You would also be entitled to recover punitive damages to punish me for my behavior.

Although the success of an action for malicious prosecution depends in part on the merits of the legal action initiated against the plaintiff, the plaintiff seeking to demonstrate that the defendant abused the legal process does not have to be concerned about the validity of any legal claims. One can maintain an action for abuse of process by showing that the defendant intentionally misused the legal process to damage the plaintiff. Abuse of process may be thought of as a way in which the defendant could seek to force the plaintiff to act contrary to his interests by threatening to initiate legal proceedings against him. If you are a reporter for the local newspaper, *The Daily Blab,* who learns that the head of my Uncle Buster has recently turned up in a gumball machine at a nearby gas station, then you might want to write a story about the discovery. However, I would probably not be very sympathetic to your plan to print an article about Uncle Buster on the society page. Because I would want to take whatever steps I could to keep my already tattered family name out of the papers, I might threaten to reveal to the police that you illegally brew orange tea in your basement. If you decided to go ahead and run the story about Uncle Buster, then my success in having legal proceedings initiated against you for illegally brewing orange tea could subject me to legal action by you for abuse of process because I sought to use my knowledge of an unrelated matter to compel you to kill the story about Uncle Buster. Because my action would amount to the civil equivalent of extortion, I would be liable to you for any damage that you could satisfactorily demonstrate had resulted from my threats to expose your quirky beverage preferences. The fact that you illegally brew orange tea would not excuse my behavior because my actions were motivated not by any desire to bring you to justice but instead by my own selfish intentions to force you to kill a story that would not be very flattering to me or my family.

Fraud

Because many people believe that the surest way to success in the business world is to bend the truth about the value of their products, consumers often need to know what they must do to establish that a particular seller has committed fraud. The prospective plaintiff seeking to maintain an action for fraud must establish that (1) the defendant made a false material statement about a past or present fact (2) with the intent of causing the plaintiff to rely on that false statement (3) and that the plaintiff justifiably relied on the false statement (4) thereby suffering damages.

The misrepresentation of fact must concern a past or present fact; one would not incur liability for misrepresentation if he made a false statement regarding a future fact. If I promised to give a harmonica concert at the municipal incinerator next week, then I would be liable for fraud only if I had no intention of performing the concert at the time I promised to do so. In such a case, I could be liable for fraud because I misrepresented my intentions at that particular point in time regarding my participation in a future event. If I was sincere when I made my promise but later changed my mind, then I would not be liable for misrepresentation because I did intend to give the concert when I originally made the promise.

Misrepresentations of fact usually consist of affirmative statements by the defendant. In general, the defendant is under no duty to disclose a material fact to the plaintiff unless he has some sort of fiduciary relationship with the plaintiff or if his statements created an erroneous impression in the plaintiff's mind that the defendant knew about but failed to correct. If I am the trustee of a fund set up by Veronica Thunderbolt, the grandmother of Dominique, then my efforts to convince Dominique to purchase an old automobile of mine, which runs only when it is hooked up to another vehicle or an ox cart, might be considered fraudulent if I failed to inform Dominique of the true condition of the vehicle. My attempt to blame the automobile's inability to move under its own power (except when rolling downhill) on a chill in the air could render me liable for misrepresentation because my fiduciary relationship with Dominique would require me to disclose to her the actual condition of the vehicle.

Misrepresentation might also be found if I turned the ignition key of my automobile and explained the absence of any noise under the hood as being due to the technological sophistication of the engine. The fact that the engine block is actually missing (due to my decision to replace it with a gigantic hamster on a wheel) would render me liable for misrepresentation because my statement suggested to Dominique that the absence of engine noise was due to my automobile's advanced technology and not the fact that it was powered solely by a rodent. Because Dominique does not know where the engine is located—much less what it is supposed to do—then my failure to correct Dominique's erroneous impression about the nature of my automobile's engine would amount to a misrepresentation of fact. Whether a person wiser in the ways of the world such as Ingrid Engebrettsen would have bothered to lift the hood and look for the engine might be relevant because one must justifiably rely on the misrepresentation to maintain an action for fraud. I could argue that Dominique should have checked whether my automobile had a working engine before she paid the purchase price. The ease with which Dominique could have verified my statement might weaken her argument of justifiable reliance even though she had no duty to investigate my statements of fact.

I must make my misrepresentations of fact knowing that they are false or with reckless disregard as to their truth or falsity. If I told Dominique that my automobile had high-performance racing tires without bothering to verify the truth of my statement, then I could be liable for misrepresentation if it was later determined that the tires were actually wooden wagon wheels. If Dominique is able to establish that I knew my statement was false or that I was reckless with regard to its veracity, then she would have to demonstrate that I intended for her to rely on my misrepresentations and that her reliance was reasonable. If Dominique decided to go ahead with the purchase based on my statement that my automobile was able to fly like a plane at twice the speed of sound, then it is doubtful that her reliance could be regarded as justified because flying cars are not generally available for sale to the public. Although substantial deference will be shown to Dominique's assertion that she was entitled to rely on my false statements of fact, she will not be entitled to rely on statements that are patently absurd. My assertion that my automobile can fly would be regarded as absurd by the average person so that Dominique's action against me would probably be dismissed.

Although people are not usually entitled to rely on false statements of opinion, liability may be found if the defendant possessed superior knowledge or skill as would be the case with a salesman who sells a specific brand of automobile such as the Carthage Roadster. A customer who knows nothing about Carthage Roadsters would arguably be justified in relying on the opinions of the salesman as they relate to that particular model; the salesman would not automatically be able to hide behind the shield of immunity usually afforded to false statements of opinion. However, the defendant's opinion would have to be reasonably specific so as to avoid having it characterized as "puffing" and it would have to be such that a reasonable person could justifiably rely on it. If the salesman declared that it was his opinion that the Carthage Roadster accelerated faster than any other automobile in its class including the famed Satyr, the fact that every article he had ever read about the Carthage Roadster had reached the opposite conclusion would suggest that the salesman had no basis for his opinion and should be held liable for any damages suffered by the customer who relied on that opinion in deciding to acquire a Carthage Roadster.

The plaintiff would have to demonstrate satisfactorily that he suffered tangible injuries due to his reliance on the false statement of fact or opinion. Because damages are not presumed to exist in such cases, the plaintiff would probably be able to recover the funds he expended in reliance on the misrepresentation less the value of the goods he received. If the plaintiff paid $5,000 for a Carthage Roadster because he believed the salesman's statement about its superior acceleration but the actual value of the car was only $4,000 due to its sluggish handling, then he should be able to recover $1,000 from the dealer.

When misrepresentations are made negligently instead of with knowledge as to their falsity or with reckless disregard for their truth, then the injured plaintiff may bring an action for negligent misrepresentation. This tort often arises when a person such as a stockbroker or an attorney (who makes her living providing information to others) negligently furnishes erroneous information to a client on which the client justifiably relies to his detriment. If you are my stockbroker and we are discussing various investments over the telephone, your statement that one of my favorite stocks, Porcine Entrails, has dropped twenty dollars that morning might prompt me to order you to sell it as quickly as possible so that I could minimize my losses. I would not be very happy to find out later that you had misread the price of the stock and that it had dropped only two points. Had I known the truth about the price of the stock, I probably would not have ordered you to sell it because a two-point drop would be well within the normal range of daily market fluctuations. My damages would probably be limited to the commission owed to you for selling the stock plus the amount above the proceeds received from the sale necessary to repurchase the stock because I would not have ordered you to sell it if you had given me the correct information about its price.

Another example of negligent misrepresentation would be if my attorney, Ian Forktongue, informed me that my town had just enacted a new ordinance making it illegal for residents to build gazebos on their property. Even though the customized lumber I had recently acquired to build a gazebo was now worthless, I might go ahead and chop the lumber into kindling for my fireplace. Despite my pecuniary loss, I would be content knowing that I had complied with the town council's latest attempt to demonstrate that its members share a single brain. I would be rather displeased to find out from a subsequent chat with Ian that the ordinance prohibited gazelles—not gazebos—and that it was still perfectly legal for me to build a gazebo on my property. Owing to the fact that I had already relied on my attorney's advice and disposed of the lumber, I could sue him for negligent misrepresentation because he provided me with incorrect information about the ordinance and I justifiably and detrimentally relied on his erroneous statements. My recovery would probably be limited to the cost of the lumber less any money I saved by using the lumber as firewood. The fact that the words *gazebo* and *gazelle* look similar when one glances at the small print of a municipal ordinance would not alter my attorney's obligation to compensate me for my loss.

Vicarious Liability

Usually when an employee commits a tortious offense within the scope of his employment, his liability will be imputed to his employer due to their working relationship. Even though the employer may have done nothing to cause the tort and had no knowledge about the circumstances resulting in the injury, he will often be held vicariously or derivatively liable for the damages caused by his employee. The doctrine of *respondeat superior* provides that employers may be vicariously liable for the actions of their employees while the employees are working on behalf of their employer. This doctrine may be extended to cover intentional torts such as battery if the employee's job requires that he sometimes use force to deal with unruly customers. If I ran a bingo parlor that was popular with the nuns at a nearby convent, I might need to employ several beefy individuals to toss out those nuns who liked to scream that the games were fixed after losing a few rounds. Even though one of my bouncers, Oaf Hedley, might use too much force and toss an unruly nun through a plate glass window, I would not be able to avoid having his liability for using excessive force against the nun imputed to me because I hired him to control the behavior of the patrons by using whatever means were necessary. As a result, the nun would be able to sue both Oaf and me for battery and recover the damages for her injuries from me.

What could I do to avoid having the liability incurred by my bouncers imputed to me? I might decide to hire an independent contractor to provide the bouncers needed to maintain order in my bingo parlor. Because these bouncers would not be my employees, then the doctrine of *respondeat superior* would not apply and I should be able to avoid having their intentional torts imputed to me. However, this immunity from derivative liability would not be upheld if I had hired the independent contractor to perform extremely dangerous duties for me such as excavation or mining. It is unclear what the result would be if the independent contractor provided me with bouncers who spent their breaks dredging fill from the lake behind my bingo parlor. In such a situation, the independent contractor would likely incur liability if his bouncers mangled any nuns, whereas I would be liable for any damages caused by their digging activities because excavation is generally regarded as an extremely dangerous activity for which the customer (me) should be responsible.

Vicarious liability may also be imputed to the partners in a partnership or the joint venturers in a joint venture. So long as a partner (joint venturer) is acting on behalf of the partnership (joint venture), the other partners (joint venturers) will be vicariously liable for any tortious offenses he commits. Before liability will attach, however, the plaintiff must demonstrate that the defendant's actions were motivated by a business purpose shared by the other members of the entity. If the defendant was involved in a car accident with another person while racing to deliver some papers from the partnership to one of its clients, then the defendant's tortious conduct would be imputed to the partnership. If the accident resulted from the defendant's spontaneous decision to drive down the sidewalk because he wanted to see the terrified looks on the faces of the pedestrians before he ran over them, then it would be difficult to argue that his actions somehow facilitated the business purpose of the entity or that the other members should be held responsible. A different outcome might result if the defendant had driven onto the sidewalk to take a shortcut so that he would be able to deliver the papers to the client on time even though his change in strategy knocked down and injured several pedestrians. In this situation, a court might determine that the defendant's primary purpose for driving onto the sidewalk was to facilitate the business of the entity by delivering the papers to the client thus necessitating that the other members be held responsible for the defendant's actions.

A parent may be vicariously liable for the torts or crimes committed by her child only if the tort or crime occurs while the child is performing some task on behalf of the parent. In general, however, the parent will not usually be held responsible for the actions of her child unless the parent stands to benefit in some tangible manner from the child's conduct. If your ten-year-old son, Rasputin, takes a skunk into a bank and threatens to spray the tellers with its scent unless they give him a big bag of money, then you would not be held responsible for the crime because Rasputin robbed the bank for his own benefit. You would be liable, however, if Rasputin was merely an agent acting on your behalf and he gave you the bag of money in exchange for some baseball cards. Because Rasputin's primary purpose in robbing the bank was to confer a financial benefit on you, his liability for his crime would be imputed to you.

Contribution and Indemnity

When the negligent actions of two or more persons cause a single indivisible injury to another person, each of the negligent parties will be jointly and severally liable for the entire injury. In situations in which it is possible to identify which defendant caused what injury, it is not necessary to hold the defendants jointly and severally liable because their respective degrees of fault can be determined. If Otto Hertz and I were out in the woods hunting for game and Otto shot his arrow and I fired my gun at what appeared to be a moose but was actually Mr. Tibbs wearing moose antlers to celebrate the coming of spring, then the extent to which each of us had caused his injury could be determined because it would be quite obvious which wound was caused by Otto's arrow and which wound by my bullet. However, Otto and I might still be held jointly and severally liable for the entire injury if the court hearing our case determined that we had acted in concert when we injured Mr. Tibbs. If we were both found to be liable for the entire injury, then Mr. Tibbs could recover the entire amount of the damages from either me or Otto if he so chose. If I paid the entire amount, then Mr. Tibbs's judgment against me would be satisfied. Mr. Tibbs would not then be able to sue Otto to inflate the amount of his recovery because he already received the entire amount of the judgment from me. My satisfaction of the judgment would require Mr. Tibbs to release me from his claim. In earlier times, Mr. Tibbs's release of me would have also served to release Otto and any other joint tortfeasors who might be responsible for his injuries. Nowadays, Mr. Tibbs would be able to avoid that result by executing a document that released me from liability but reserved any rights he might have to proceed against Otto.

When two or more defendants are found to be jointly and severally liable for the injuries suffered by the plaintiff, then the recovery of the full judgment by the plaintiff from one of the defendants will give the paying defendant the right to seek contribution from the other defendants. If I paid the entire judgment to Mr. Tibbs, then I would be entitled to bring an action against Otto to compel him to pay me for his pro rata share of the judgment. Assuming that we were both found to be equally at fault for the injury we caused to Mr. Tibbs, then I would be entitled to seek half of the judgment from Otto as contribution.

Indemnification, by contrast, involves shifting the entire burden of the judgment from one defendant to another and often arises in situations in which an employee has committed a tort while in the scope of his employment. If Otto negligently ran over a bicyclist while driving to Garden World to pick up some shovels and hoes, then the bicyclist would probably sue both me and Otto for her injuries because Otto was driving the truck while in my employment. If the somewhat flattened bicyclist was awarded a judgment against both of us, then I might seek indemnification for the full amount of the judgment from Otto because I had nothing to do with his running over the bicyclist and was certainly not at fault for Otto's negligence. If I was successful, then I would be able to obtain whatever portion of the judgment I paid to the bicyclist from Otto. My suit for indemnification would completely shift the burden of paying the judgment to Otto. I could also demonstrate that I was entitled to be indemnified if my employment contract with Otto contained a clause providing that he would indemnify me for any funds that I was obligated to pay due to his negligent conduct. In such a case, it should be a fairly straightforward procedure to go to court and request that a judge enter an order to enforce the agreement.

Wrongful Death Actions

The phrase *wrongful death* has nothing to do with whether a particular person deserved to die but instead refers to the rights of a deceased person's spouse or personal representative to bring a tort action on his behalf. Traditionally, any claim that could be brought by a victim against the tortfeasor was extinguished with the death of either the victim or the wrongdoer. However, many states have enacted survival laws that permit such claims to be brought by the executor of the decedent's estate or the appropriate family member. The plaintiff in a wrongful death action may recover damages for loss of consortium, medical and funeral expenses, and loss of support (lost wages). However, the plaintiff may not recover any damages to compensate the beneficiaries for the pain and suffering of the decedent because such damages would be impossible to calculate as the decedent is no longer available to answer questions about his physical and emotional injuries.

Because a wrongful death action proceeds as though the decedent were still alive, a defendant may raise any defenses to defeat a wrongful death action that would have defeated the claim if the decedent was alive such as his assumption of risk or contributory negligence. My gardener, Otto Hertz, could bring a wrongful death action on behalf of his brother, Karl, who was crushed to death when the circus fat man, Dave Dirigible (whom Karl was trying to photograph), slipped and fell on top of him. Otto would be able to proceed with the suit only if Karl himself could have sued Dave for injuring him. Unfortunately, Otto might be unable to recover anything because Dave could argue that Karl had knowingly and voluntarily assumed the risks associated with standing in close proximity to a circus fat man. Alternatively, Dave could try to establish that Karl was contributorily negligent because he positioned himself in such a way that any sudden movement by Dave would cause Karl to be buried beneath an avalanche of pink flesh. Even if Dave was unable to raise any defenses against a wrongful death action by Otto on Karl's behalf, he would still be able to prevent Otto from recovering any damages as Karl's beneficiary if Otto himself was contributory negligent. If Otto had pushed Karl into Dave and thus caused Dave to fall on top of Karl, then the fact that Otto was the one responsible for the accident could bar him from recovering any damages. The outcome would necessarily depend on the extent to which Otto's conduct contributed to Karl's death.

Family and Governmental Tort Immunities

Family members have traditionally been denied the opportunity to sue one another in tort due to the widespread concern that such a right would be misused and would destroy many families. Many states have eliminated the immunity from suit afforded to spouses so that husbands and wives can now bring actions in tort against each other. This means that the husband and wife who used to enjoy flinging the everyday dishes at each other with impunity will now have to be more careful because he or she could be sued if he or she beaned the other with an errant plate. Although spouses are now free to air their grievances against each other in court, most states have refused to permit children to sue their parents in tort. The vitality of this particular concept of tort immunity is probably bolstered by the belief of many legislators that there are tens of thousands of children waiting on the sidelines to sue their parents for the pain and suffering they endured because they were forced to wear secondhand clothes and drive domestic automobiles. The immunity afforded to family members, however, has always been limited in that it will not shield persons who commit intentional torts against other family members nor will it bar suits by or against relatives outside the immediate family such as aunts, uncles, nieces, nephews, cousins, and grandparents.

Third persons who interfere with the sanctity of the marital relationship (by keeping one of the spouses warm when the other spouse is not around) may be sued for damages by the aggrieved spouse. Claims for loss of consortium and marital services most often arise when one spouse has committed adultery. Either spouse may also recover damages from a third party whose negligent conduct has injured the other spouse and resulted in a loss of consortium and marital services. As far as children are concerned, a parent may maintain an action for the loss of the child's services when the child's injury is caused by the defendant's negligent or intentional tortious conduct. However, children are generally not permitted to maintain actions to recover damages from tortfeasors who intentionally or negligently injure their parents.

Governmental immunities are somewhat more mundane than love affairs, but they must be considered if one decides to file a claim against the federal government or any state or municipal agency. The doctrine of sovereign immunity has historically prevented people from filing actions against the federal government except when it explicitly consented to be sued for particular causes of action. As a result, the plaintiff may be forced to fit her particular claim against the government into one of the specified exceptions. Although the courts have tended to expand the rights of plaintiffs to sue the federal government in recent years, potential litigants continue to be barred from filing claims for such things as assault, battery, or false imprisonment because any success with such claims could greatly hinder the government's ability to enforce its laws and preserve domestic order. In general, however, a person may file a claim only with regard to those governmental actions that are ministerial (administrative) in nature as opposed to those actions that may be characterized as discretionary.

Although the immunity afforded to municipalities has been eroded more severely in recent years than that enjoyed by the federal government or most state governments, a plaintiff seeking to sue a municipality will not often be able to maintain a cause of action based on the improper performance by municipal employees of a government function such as police or fire services. However, the municipality will not be protected from suit when it engages in conduct that may be characterized as proprietary as opposed to governmental such as being an equity partner in a local office building. The test for differentiating between the two spheres of activity is whether the activity is one that is traditionally carried out by municipalities alone (such as whipping jaywalkers) or if it is an activity in which private entities have also participated (such as building and maintaining municipal parking lots). The presumption that a particular activity is proprietary in nature will be strengthened if the city derives some tangible benefit such as user fees from the activity. If the activity can be characterized as proprietary, then the plaintiff will be able to sue the municipality as he would any private defendant.

INDEX

Index

Index

Index

Index

Index

Index

Index

Index

Index

Index

Index

Index

Index